"None of us are beyond the need or the reach of God's grace. Michael English's story is a profound and timely celebration of this great truth. Indeed, God's name is Redeemer . . . he restores broken things and broken people. This is the heart of the gospel. I sat with Michael and looked into his eyes the day after his public exposure, and I sat with Michael recently and looked again into his eyes. Darkness has given way to light—The Light of the World. Michael is a changed and changing man, and there is only one explanation: Jesus has come to make all things new. Read this book and reconsider how dangerous it is to write off anyone."

—Scotty Smith, Founding pastor, Christ Community Church, Franklin, Tennessee

"It saddens me when the church finds more pleasure in gossiping about our fallen brothers and sisters than in celebrating their restoration to wholeness. We should all celebrate that Michael English is healed, restored, and renewed by the cross—a cross that is for you and for me, for forgiveness, and for the mending of broken vessels."

—Michael W Smith, Musician

"Michael's life is a beautiful picture of God's forgiveness and restoration. He is a new creation. The old has passed away and all things are new—and Michael has an amazing story to tell."

—Mark Hall, Lead singer, Casting Crowns

"Before the prodigal came home, Luke's Gospel says he first 'came to himself.' Years ago Michael faced the same dilemma many young, mega-talented people face: because of his natural gifts he, unfortunately, 'came to us' before he had 'come to himself.' The results were predictable and horribly painful. As his friend and pastor, I've spent the last thirteen years watching him slowly and truly 'come to himself.' Now as he makes his way back from the far country and home to ministry, I pray we will receive him as well and wisely as the Father has. Indeed, he has taken the long way home. His journey has taught him a lot. It has much to teach us."

—Stan Mitchell, Pastor, GracePointe Church, Brentwood, Tennessee

"I am one of the biggest Michael English fans there is. When my father passed away, it was Michael's music that got me through. I believe with all of my heart that God has given Michael the opportunity to continue ministering to the hurting. Through His trials and victories, Michael celebrates the God of second chances, and believe me, that is the God that all of us need to intimately know."

—Bart Marshall Millard, Lead singer, Mercy Me

"What a wonderful story of restoration and redemption—the kind of work that God wants to do in all of us, if we will but let him. Thanks, Michael, for openly and honestly telling about your life, your struggles, your successes, your failures and, ultimately, your faith and hope in a God who redeems. The change He has brought about in you is nothing short of amazing. . . . Welcome home!"\

—Neal Joseph, Executive Pastor, Fellowship Bible Church,
Brentwood, Tennessee, and former President of Warner Alliance

"The pain, suffering, and alienation Michael has experienced by his own doing and at the hands of others would all amount to nothing except for the fact that in Christ alone God has rescued Michael from the vicious downward spiral of addiction and depression and has restored him in order that his life would be a testimony of God's life-transforming grace."

—Frank Reich, Former quarterback, Buffalo Bills

"Michael English writes that singing is his worship, and I believe that every time I hear him sing. His book is also a song of worship. It's a song of hope. It's a call to each one of us to hold onto God and to never give up, because God never lets go and He never gives up on us. Michael's book is a reminder that God will meet us wherever we are—in fact He will run to meet us—and His love will always guide us home. Now that's something to sing about!"

—Mark Miller, Lead singer, Sawyer Brown

+ the prodigal comes home +

+ the prodigal comes home +

My Story of Failure and
God's Story of Redemption

Michael English

With Lynn Vincent

THOMAS NELSON
Since 1798

thomasnelson.com

Published in Nashville, Tennesse, by Thomas Nelson, Inc.

Thomas Nelson, Inc. titles may be purchased in bulk for educational, business, fund-raising, or sales promotional use. For information, please e-mail SpecialMarkets@ThomasNelson.com.

All Scripture quotations, unless otherwise indicated, are taken from The Holy Bible, New International Version (NIV). Copyright © 1973, 1978, 1984. International Bible Society. Used by permission of Zondervan Bible Publishers.

Other Scripture references are from The King James Version of the Bible (KJV)

Although this is a work of nonfiction, some of the names have been changed.

Editorial Staff: Greg Daniel, acquisition editor, and Thom Chittom, managing editor
Cover Design: Gilbert & Carlson
Page Design: Kay Meadows

Library of Congress Cataloging-in-Publication Data

English, Michael.
    The prodigal comes home / Michael English, with Lynn Vincent.
      p. cm.
    ISBN 13: 978-0-8499-0173-7
    ISBN 10: 0-8499-0173-1
    1. English, Michael. 2. Contemporary Christian musicians–United
States–Biography. I. Vincent, Lynn. II. Title.

ML420.E64A3 2007
782.25092–dc22
[B]

2006101023

Printed in the United States of America

07 08 09 10 11 12 QW 9 8 7 6 5 4 3 2 1

+

I would like to dedicate this book to my wife Marcie, and my children Megan, Bella, and my son-in-law Keith.
You are the reason why I was able to complete this book.
Without you, there wouldn't have been a happy ending.
Jesus, thank you for second chances.

+

+ foreword +
by Bill Gaither

I have lived and worked in the world of artistry for about fifty years now, and if there is one thing I have learned about artists it is this: most artists do not come in neat little packages. The giftedness that launches an artist into the spotlight is often the very thing that brings the most torment into their lives. Original artistry—true genius—is a gift of God. It is not saved for the perfect. It is also most certainly not saved for the self-confident. But the coach and teacher inside me always wants to salvage that gift when I see it in someone.

Michael English is one such artist—a body made of flesh with a supernatural gift. He came to us in 1989, and I was drawn by the passion in his voice as I listened to a tape of him singing. This was not the first time I had seen raw talent like this, and I knew there was great potential inside this young man. When I met him face to face, I was taken with his humble, quiet spirit. I felt very strongly that this was an artist the world needed to hear.

When Michael started singing with the Gaither Vocal Band, audiences connected with him immediately and he became the voice around which our sound was centered. His powerful delivery and commanding presence were truly remarkable. Off-stage I began to see chinks in his armor. But anytime I needed to address concerns I had, Michael was never defensive. He was open to correction and, I believe, appreciated it.

foreword

One concern I had was the result of a chemical imbalance that Michael battled which caused severe anxiety attacks. When these attacks came on, I knew this was way over my head so I encouraged him to find professional help. One night in Arizona, after one of these attacks had reached a level at which he could not function, I sat beside his bed all night and watched him struggle. I was concerned that he would not make it through the night. Yet as he struggled, I saw a young man who felt responsible for the predicament he had left me in. He said he was afraid he had let me down.

"You didn't let me down," I reassured him.

By some miracle, he was on-stage with us the next night. During "It Is Finished" he sang his verse as powerfully as he ever had:

Yet in my heart the battle was raging;
Not all pris'ners of war have come home.
These were battlefields of my own making;
I didn't know that the war had been won.

I knew what he had been through the night before, and it was unbelievable that he could stand and sing those words which very much described the battle raging inside him.

While Michael was still singing with the Vocal Band, another record label approached with the possibility of becoming a solo artist. For a while he was able to maintain his solo work while traveling with us, but the time finally came when I saw that he was ready to launch out on his own. His solo career was growing quite rapidly. I remember the night at a hotel in Alabama when I asked him if he thought it was time that he should leave.

He was reluctant. "I don't want to leave you in a hole."

"Michael, you have worked hard and you've given it your best," I reminded him. "Go with my blessing."

We held a joint press release and he departed the Gaither Vocal Band amicably. A few weeks later, Gloria and I went to see him sing in his solo concert in Fort Wayne and, to be honest, he was quite stunning. As I watched the overwhelming response he was getting from audiences, I was both excited and fearful.

"God protect him," I would silently pray.

That year he was nominated for numerous Dove Awards by the Gospel Music Association. The Saturday before the award ceremony I got a call from a friend who said, "Michael is in trouble and I think it is about to become public."

The next night, Michael asked to meet with Gloria and me on the bus. He said, "I haven't told you the truth. I have really messed up." He began to confess to us his life and the decisions that had put him in a really difficult situation.

We talked for awhile then Gloria prayed for him. I still remember that prayer very well. She asked God to take what Satan had intended for evil and destruction and use it to ultimately redeem him.

A couple days later the damaging news was everywhere. I made it clear to Michael that I was still his friend. We stayed in touch as much as possible, but communication with him became more difficult. I spoke with Michael's wife Lisa a few times and I knew he was on a confusing roller coaster. His choices were causing a domino effect of consequences, one piling onto the next. While I know Michael would have given anything to be able to go back and redo everything, that was not an option. So it was two steps forward and three steps backward for awhile.

In 1999 we invited him to come to a Homecoming taping, where he sang "Lord, Feed Your Children." At the place he was in his journey, this was a song I felt that he could honestly sing:

My vessel is empty, though once I had plenty,
My soul is barren and dry
Somewhere flows a Fountain beyond a distant mountain,
Let me drink from the River of Life

Lord, feed Your children as we stand here waiting
To eat from the table of life;
Drink from the Fountain that flows from the mountain,
Let me feast from the Father's supply

foreword

So long I have hungered; no man could number
The days that I've longed to be,
In a land filled with honey, where the rivers are runnin';
Very soon now will I taste and see.

Southern gospel legend Vestal Goodman was there, along with a host of other artists who loved him, and they received him as a child of God. And while I would like to say he was out of the woods for good, this was not entirely the case. However, since that time I have seen Michael make huge strides toward wholeness. The man I see today is one who desires to learn from his mistakes. He has allowed the fallout of past failures to fuel his desire to keep progressing. I believe he is a man who is truly seeking God's best.

I could never stop believing that inside this broken, fragile life was the heart of a good young man. I had seen his best and his worst, and I knew that the Michael English God could use was still in there somewhere.

We are all just pilgrims in process; we don't come neatly packaged. We are complex and tortured by our best traits much of the time. Some artists' frailties are less obvious; others are exposed at the highest possible level. But the good news of the gospel is that there is forgiveness for every sin and there is a bright future for those who keep getting up after each fall, asking for forgiveness, and starting on a spiritual pilgrimage toward wholeness. Michael kept getting up. And today, it is a joy to see God redeeming those mistakes for His glory. To me, there is nothing better to sing about. And if anyone can sing about that redemption with authority, it is my friend Michael English.

+ introduction +

Ten thousand spiders dropped from my hairline, circled my neck, crawled down my arms, and skittered across my belly. Their hateful legs pricked my skin like needles. I prayed, *Godmakeitstop, Godmakeitstop, Godmakeitstop, Godmakeitstop.* My skin poured sweat, soaking the pillow and bedsheet, but I shivered under a thick pile of blankets as pain shot through my legs, every nerve ending sparking like white fire. I twisted and moaned, bicycling against the cold, slick sheet, but the fires wouldn't go out. The ache in my legs pounded deep into my bones, cracking my sanity like hammer blows.

Sweat poured over the spiders, streaming down my neck, drenching my back. But chills racked my body, and I wished Rita, the nurse, would bring another blanket. Alone, I opened my eyes to a dark room. I couldn't see the big, round classroom clock and thanked God. I didn't want to see its mean, greedy hands holding back time, refusing to move. A cramp seized my gut and squeezed, squeezed, then burned. Vomit shot to the base of my throat and hovered there, threatening. I feared death but hoped it would come soon.

Then suddenly: salvation! Like houselights coming up slowly, the black room brightened. And above me, I saw the big, white ceiling tiles begin to rain.

Easter-colored raindrops slipped down through the tiles like ghosts through a wall and fell toward me. The drops were in the shape of pills. Painkillers! Yellow Norcos, blue Loritabs, little cream-colored Oxycontins, and best of all, the big, green Oxy 80s, my favorites. Circles, ovals, caplets, thousands and thousands of pills showered down, never ending. I knew they were real, because I could read the pharmaceutical names and numbers on them, plain as a newspaper.

Suddenly the pain in my legs erupted into flames. But if I could have just one of the falling pills, the fire, the vomit, the spiders would all go away. With both arms, I reached up into the rain and grabbed for an Oxy 80, but it melted through my fingers. I tried to catch a Loritab, another Oxy, anything, hands clasping and clenching but coming up empty. The pills were *right there*, but the rain was coming down fast and the pills were somehow hard to catch. I shouldn't have swallowed the last of my stash all at once before detox. I knew that, but now there were these pills sprinkling all around me, and all I needed was *one*. I stretched and snatched at the pastel raindrops. There were so many, so many! *Just one* and this would all be better.

But the pills fell right through my hands and disappeared into the pile of blankets. Why! Why couldn't I catch one?

Grief burst in my brain like a bomb as I realized the pills weren't real, only another hallucination. The false rain faded away, and reality replaced it: I was a junkie in a lockdown. A man without hope, clinging to the pitiful end of a ruined life.

I HAD RUINED IT MYSELF. In the years before the pill rain, I had been living what some people would consider a dream. God had blessed me with a gift for singing, and it appeared to the world that I was using my gift to glorify Him, to lift up believers and bring the message of hope to the lost. As a member of the Gaither Vocal Band, I had won Grammy Awards. Between 1992 and 1994, the Gospel Music Association had loaded me down with so many Dove Awards, I couldn't carry them all. On the outside, I had it going on: I was married to a gorgeous woman and was father to a daughter who was the jewel of my life. I was wealthy, famous, and a friend of the famous. I lived in a designer house. I didn't even carry my own suitcases.

And yet you may be wondering, *Who is Michael English?*

The fact that you don't know—or may not have heard from me in a while—testifies to this truth: God is not mocked.

On the outside, I was flying high. But inside I was an empty shell and a traitor to my family. I had tossed aside the finest gifts God had given me and, like the wandering son in the prodigal story, had strayed far from home, looking to fill the hole in my soul. But, as with the prodigal son, God Himself had already provided me with the path to healing—put it right under my nose. But I was too vain and desperate, too shallow in my faith and high on myself to see it.

The world saw it in May 1994:

Newsweek: "Scandal touches the exploding world of Christian pop. . . ."

Associated Press Wire: "Just a week after being named gospel music's Artist of the Year, Michael English has been dropped by his record label. . . ."

The Tennessean: "Gospel star Michael English yesterday returned symbols of his success—his six Dove Awards—as First Call moved to replace Marabeth Jordan, the singer with whom English has conceived a child."

I had become a hypocrite, something I had hated more than anything since I was a little boy performing Southern gospel in the little country churches of North Carolina. I had shamed the name of Christ in front of the whole world, giving more ammunition to people who think that Christianity is a joke. But the world didn't see what happened after that. My public fall from grace opened a trapdoor into a private hell.

If I were the only person with a private hell, this wouldn't be a book worth reading. But over the last few years, I have learned I'm not alone. When I was famous, I sang in enormous auditoriums, and my management team was considering booking me next on an arena tour. Today I'm singing in churches again and telling my story, just like I did as a boy. And hardly a time goes by when someone doesn't come up to me afterward and say, "I know what you went through, because I'm going through it right now."

This is a book about the God who walks through the fire with us — a confounding, wise, compassionate, mysterious God of grace and mercy. In my life, His mercy was not shaped in a single white-light moment, a Damascus Road experience, in which He shouted down from heaven, "You are healed!" and I got up and started walking the straight and narrow and testifying to my miracle. Today I believe that's true of most people, and that's why I wrote this book.

In today's world of instant everything, we often want the road to healing to be like a Damascus expressway—no potholes, no surprises, no stops along the way. For me, the road was more like a rugged mountain trail that wound around blind curves so that I couldn't see too far ahead. Sometimes I slipped entirely off the trail and bloodied myself on the way down into a ditch.

Growing up in North Carolina, I spent Sundays in churches where, if you were a Christian in sin, you might as well have your mail forwarded to hell. And if you were going to be *healed*, it was because you had faith to *believe* it. (Can I get an "Amen"?) And if you weren't healed, it was because you didn't have enough faith. But you don't have to go to that kind of church to lose the hope of healing. Today there are thousands of people sitting in church pews every Sunday who look like they've got it together on the outside but are broken on the inside. Who wants to grab a Christian brother or sister by the shoulders and shout, "I'm *not* together! I'm in trouble! My relationship with God is terrible! I feel like a fake!" Instead, they pass out another bulletin or stack another chair, afraid to reach out, because everyone else looks like they have life's problems whipped.

My problem was drug addiction. But there is a long list of other obsessions that pull us away from God: work, success, material possessions; beauty, fitness, trying to stay young; pornography, sex, someone else's spouse. Even ministry can stand in the way of the life God wants for us.

Maybe especially ministry. I had a terrific ministry. My first album sold two hundred fifty thousand copies. My face was on the cover of magazines.

And in the pages of those magazines, people read what I had to say about God. I was the "celebrity" face for a pro-life group. I sang with Dolly Parton, crossing over between Christian and country. I sang at an astronaut's funeral, spreading the gospel to the worlds of science and government. After Buffalo Bills quarterback Frank Reich engineered the biggest comeback in NFL history, he went on national television and read aloud the words to my song "In Christ Alone," so that millions of football fans across America heard the message. It was said of me, "If ever a man feels the calling to live by the words of his own music, it is Michael English."

Oh—and I was cheating on my wife.

I WANT TO SAY RIGHT UP FRONT that this is not an "I'm sorry I had an affair; now please buy my records" book. And it is not the Christian rendition of *VH1 Behind the Music*, where an artist sells a bunch of records, gets cocky, womanizes, becomes an addict, cleans up, and sells some more records. This book is about a God who refused to let a man destroy himself. Who reached down to rescue me even when I was literally wallowing in my own filth. Who saved me so that I could tell others.

Even those who know me know only part of my story. In 2000 there came a time when I actually crawled on my knees and begged God, out loud, to either rescue me or let me die.

Let me tell you what He did.

+ chapter one +

Inside Temple Baptist Church in Detroit, Michigan, the band First Call hit their last note, darkness dropped over the massive sanctuary like a blanket, and thirty-five hundred people erupted into cheers. Working by penlight, an expert crew swept onstage and shuffled equipment while whistles and shouts echoed in the huge hall. Waiting backstage with my band, I could hear calls from the crowd—"Michael! . . . Michael!"—then scattered whistling and the hushed restlessness of a crowd waiting for a headline act.

It was the spring of 1994, the opening show on tour for my second solo album, *Hope.* By then I'd had three number one hits on the Christian adult contemporary charts. I had won five Dove Awards, including Male Vocalist of the Year for two years running. I'd been with the Grammy-winning Gaither Vocal Band for nine years. I'd sung with the *Young Messiah* tour, the most successful Christian musical production of all time. We'd even sung at the White House for Bill and Hillary Clinton.

The *Hope* tour was already sold out for months down the line. Fan response was so enthusiastic that when we pulled up to a venue in the tour bus, I had to keep my head down to get into the building without being seen. Otherwise, a crowd would come running.

Also, I was making *a lot* of money.

As a music style, Christian contemporary music, also known as CCM, was entering its third decade as a multimillion-dollar industry. My manager,

1

the prodigal comes home

Norman Miller, was one of its pioneers, handling singers like Twila Paris and, later, Avalon and Casting Crowns. He had put together an incredible show: I was touring with my good friend Mark Lowry, the well-known funny man of the Gaither Vocal Band. A newer group, Angelo and Veronica, was the opening act. And the group First Call had replaced Mel Tunney with a new singer, Marabeth Jordan; *Hope* was their comeback tour.

Norman is right when he says today that the *Hope* tour was "magical." My management team, including my record label, Warner Alliance, had decided to pull out all the stops, making the show a true production. On tour for my first album, *Michael English*, I'd sung with performance tracks. This time we held auditions for a band and put together an amazing group of musicians, including the accomplished drummer David Huff. David also served as musical director for the tour and had programmed a spectacular light show with lasers and blazing spots synchronized with the musical buildup that preceded my entrance.

I remember that night in Detroit like it happened an hour ago. I had been singing in front of folks for most of my life, but when I stepped out on that stage, it was beyond anything someone like me, an ignorant fool from Wallace, North Carolina, ever could have dreamed.

The moment the stage was set, technicians triggered the audio intro and a low hum broke into the darkness. The crowd began to stir again, whistling, clapping, shouting out. Still no lights.

The low hum rose, then broke into a musical "punch"—keyboards—at the same split second that multicolored lasers blazed through the sanctuary. Then darkness again. The crowd went crazy. Another punch—brass—and violet lasers raked the stage. Darkness. A guitar riff flashed blue. Snares lit the stage red. Between the laser flashes, the stage was still black and the crowd noise began building, building.

The band and I had rehearsed over and over getting into position on-stage in total darkness. Stepping carefully over power cords taped to the floor, the band, along with First Call, who was singing backup, quietly lined up in the wings. I stood at the back of the line, off stage left. For five minutes, we hid there as lasers and music popped over the crowd. Suddenly the sanctuary went completely black, but the music swelled, just strings. The band had only twenty seconds to slip quietly into place. They stood onstage still as statues, heads down, and then: flash! Blazing white spots hit each member of the band. The crowd roared, then the sanctuary went black.

Techs had placed a huge white spotlight at the back of the stage. I had ten seconds to get into position. A stagehand led me out. I stood center stage, back to the crowd. A building rumble of percussions, keys, and bass filled the hall. A tech flipped a switch, and the spotlight hit me, wrapped around me, and beamed toward the crowd. The effect was silhouette, with rays shooting out from my body.

The crowd screamed. And kept screaming. The sound was *so loud*, like it wasn't even real. So loud it approached distortion. I had only heard a crowd that loud once before, at a rock concert, when I went to see the group Chicago. Yet this screaming was for me. I was thinking, *Oh man, I have* made *it! This is everything I dreamed of and more.* It was overwhelming. I mean that: Over. Whelming.

We broke into "Save Me," a driving pop song:

> *The sky is full of stars tonight.*
> *But I need more than a fleeting light*
> *To take me through the night.*

It's hard to describe the crowd's reaction without sounding like my ego is huge. (It was getting huge back then, but God took care of that.) This wasn't like a Christian concert; I'd been to and performed at literally hundreds of those, maybe thousands. This was like a rock concert. It was like I could do no wrong. Even if I hit a bad note, the people were still screaming. Just going crazy. The crowd was, as they say in Southern gospel, "throwing babies out of the balconies."

I ended the first set with "Message of Mercy," a bluesy, shuffle-beat hit. Then I did a "Cher"—changed clothes—and came back with "Always for You," a pop number with a Sting vibe. We ended the second set with my number one hit "In Christ Alone," then came back for an encore with "A Place Called Hope."

After the show, I had to just . . . *leave.*

the prodigal comes home

Before the *Hope* tour, a security team would normally take me out where the fans were so that I could sign CDs and photos and T-shirts. But now there was no way to accommodate the crowds without upsetting people. There wasn't enough product to sell or enough time to sell it, then sign it. And I couldn't really go out where the crowds were anyway, because it had gotten to the point that the sixteen- to twenty-two-year-olds were, as Norman tells it today, "going nuts." The girls would do that "Omigosh-there-he-is-I-can't-breathe!" thing.

It's hard to explain the mixed feelings that kind of response created in me. One part of me honestly felt like a superstar. But another part of me couldn't understand what all the fuss was about. The truth was, I was sure that at any second somebody was going to figure it out: I wasn't talented. This dream-life was all going to come crashing down because people would figure out that I was a lazy and stupid fake, that I couldn't do anything—including sing—as well as I thought I could.

That was the message I got growing up, and it was a message that stayed with me. No matter how successful and famous I became, inside I was the little boy who still carried like an anchor the message I'd heard growing up: "He'll never amount to anything."

+ chapter two +

In the part of North Carolina where I grew up, tobacco fields covered the land like a checkerboard. Roads that were mostly dirt wound past towns that were really no more than wide places in the road that you'd miss if you blinked while driving through—places with names like Turkey, Pin Hook, and Outlaws Bridge. I mainly grew up near Wallace, in a little town called North East, a batch of houses, trailers, and tobacco fields so small it didn't even rate a name, just a direction.

My daddy, Aubine, and my mama, Grace Elizabeth, raised my brother, Biney, and me. We grew up around country folk who rounded the *a*s and *o*s at the ends of words into *r*s, and trailed off their sentences before they finished them.

"How's yer 'baccer comin'?" one farmer might ask another about his tobacco crop in the spring.

"Fair to middlin'," the other farmer would say. "I wish't it rain, though, 'cause this durn heat mumble-mumble-mumble . . ." And the farmer doing the asking would shake his head sympathetically, knowing just what the tobacco farmer meant.

The first home we lived in was a small wooden box in a tiny town called Warsaw. But when I was about six, we moved into a single-wide trailer on the property of my Aunt Annie and Uncle Fluff in North East. The trailer, with its end to the road, sat right up under a giant pecan tree. I hated that tree

5

because every summer it rained nuts all over the trailer's metal roof and made a racket like those windup monkeys you see beating sticks on a drum. I was the lucky one who had to climb on top of the trailer and sweep off all the pecans.

About a mile and a half down the road sat my Daddy's parents' house, a one-story white clapboard with a screened-in porch across the front. I spent a lot of time there. My grandparents' names were Margaret and Dewey, but everyone, even us grandkids, called them Ma English and Daddy Dewey.

Ma English was a tough old cookie. She was a short farmwife who wore her salt-and-pepper hair tied back in a tight bun, and she favored plain, checked housedresses and sturdy shoes except on Sundays. When Ma English went to church, she wore a pastel polyester dress and had a vinyl pocketbook dangling from her arm, the kind with a single gold clasp that snaps open and shut at the top. Every Sunday Ma English and Daddy Dewey sat in the same pew at North East Pentecostal Free Will Baptist Church. I remember seeing Ma English's thick, bare knees over the tops of her nylon hose because they didn't come up all the way.

Somewhere inside, my grandmother had a tender heart, but I rarely saw it. I mainly remember her no-nonsense side, like the time her son, my uncle Freddy, was beating up on Biney in Ma English's backyard. Biney was only about twelve at the time, and Uncle Freddy was a big, bruising teenager. When Biney hollered for help, Ma English simply opened up the mudroom door and, with the accuracy of a major league pitcher, beaned Freddy in the foot with a glass Coke bottle. Freddy jumped off Biney with a holler and hopped off to nurse his wound. Ma English never said a word, just shut the door again as if she'd only been checking the weather.

Another time, I was in the garden pulling weeds with Ma English when she suddenly stood up.

"Whoo-ooo," she said mildly, then held out her hand to reveal a long, brown snake dangling from it, its fangs buried in her palm. That snake may as well have been a ladybug for all the attention Ma English paid it. With a flick of her wrist, she flung it away into some bushes, then stooped over and kept right on weeding.

Daddy Dewey was just as tough. A tall man who wore thick horn-rimmed glasses, he didn't approve of rock music, women wearing pants, or anyone wearing shorts or a bathing suit. Above all, Daddy Dewey did not tolerate long hair on men. Not only did he not like the new hippie styles, he thought long-haired men weren't good for business. You see, Daddy Dewey had cornered the market on the barbering trade in North East and operated a little one-chair shop he'd opened up inside the feed mill Uncle Fluff owned. It was a fact of life that Granddaddy cut everybody's hair in town—especially *family* hair. The first time Biney drove the forty miles into Wilmington to have his hair cut in *layers,* then actually *blow dried,* I thought Daddy Dewey would have to be hospitalized.

He himself had a full head of silver hair streaked with charcoal gray. He wore it the way a lot of older men did in the 1960s—first combed down straight, then slicked over the ears on the sides and flipped back at the forehead with a dab of Brylcreem. When Daddy Dewey cut folks' hair, he always wore black slacks and a white, short-sleeved button-up shirt. He was a little overweight and one of those fellows who carried all his extra pounds in his belly. Now, a man like that can wear his belt in one of two ways—either below his belly or above his belly button. The low-riding method is risky: if a man misses a belt loop, he could be walking along and have his britches drop right down to his ankles like an elevator car. That kind of risk didn't sit well with Daddy Dewey, of course, so his belt circled him somewhere north of his navel. On workdays I thought he looked a little like Humpty-Dumpty armed with barbering shears.

Every day at five in the afternoon, my grandparents would sit out in metal rockers on their screened-in porch. You could set your clock by the Englishes sitting out. Most Southerners reading this book will know that "sitting out" means you park on the porch and watch the fireflies spark or listen to the crickets sing while you chat about the neighbors and the weather. The strange thing about my grandparents was that they didn't chat. Instead, they watched.

+ chapter three +

When I got a little older, we moved into a double-wide trailer across the street from my grandparents. "Be careful, now," my mama would say, "Ma English and Daddy Dewey are out there watching."

So I'd take care not to be caught wearing shorts or with my hair touching my ears. Or worse, lying out in the sun in a bathing suit, which my granddaddy would've thought was both shameful *and* lazy. Once, I thought about pulling my clothes off and running around the yard naked just to get it over with. Maybe Ma English and Daddy Dewey would think it couldn't get any worse than that and quit watching me.

Sometimes I'd go over and sit out with my silent grandparents, listening to the *creak-creak* of their rockers on the wooden porch. They never said a word to me or to each other. That is, until one evening when Ma English began to count.

"One . . . two . . . three . . . four . . ." Ma English said, watching the road. "Five . . . six . . . seven . . . eight . . ."

She kept on counting until she got to twenty. Then she spoke up in a sour voice. "Look, Dewey. I done counted twenty cars in the last couple of minutes," she said irritably, as if there wasn't a living soul outside her screened-in porch who had a lick of sense. "Where's everybody goin'?"

Those were the only words I ever heard spoken on the porch. But I heard other things, including one that changed me forever. Somehow, when I was about twelve or thirteen, something Daddy Dewey said filtered back across the road to Mama and Daddy's double-wide.

"He'll never amount to anything," my grandfather said, referring to me. The chain of custody on this remark is a little fuzzy today, but I suspect that Daddy Dewey told Ma English who told Daddy who told Mama who, in a moment of family feuding, repeated it to me. However they made their way across the road, those words stuck with me, forming one layer of the self-doubt that plagued me all my life.

As stern as Ma English and Daddy Dewey were, my mama's mama, Elizabeth Torans, was that full of fun. She and my granddaddy Ellis lived in Wallace, where I'd lived as a little boy. They had a white clapboard house with dark green shutters, shaded by what seemed like a whole forest of ancient pines. I never heard as much laughter in one place as I heard in that cozy old home.

Granny was a tall woman, not chubby at all, but big-boned and solid. In my memory she always had silver hair, a quick smile, and the thickest glasses I've ever seen. Nearly blind, she had to wear them even to get from room to room in her own house. It was at Granny's house that I wrote my first song, "Please Come After Me," sitting at her piano, an old upright with smooth, spidery cracks in the ivory keys and a tinny sound that was slightly out of tune. I wasn't more than thirteen, but I was already long like a string bean, sitting on a little three-legged stool that rose when you twisted it. Granny had been the church pianist for years, and she inspired me, pounding out hymns like "Blessed Assurance" and "Victory in Jesus" and belting out the lyrics in her warbling soprano. As I built my singing career, Granny was my biggest fan. If I had a concert within two or three hours of her home, she'd be there on that designated family row, looking proud. Most of the time, my mama, Grace, and her sister, my aunt Linda, would be the ones to drive Granny to my concerts. On the way, the three of them liked to cut up in the car.

One time, they were driving out to see me in Nashville. When they rolled into town in traffic, Granny, sitting in the backseat, said, "Look here, Grace."

When Mama turned around, Granny was staring out the window at the man driving in the next car, her dentures pushed halfway out and her Coke-bottle glasses pulled out far enough to make her eyeballs look huge. The other driver was so freaked out, he ran a stoplight to get away. Granny thought that was a hoot.

Granddaddy Ellis was just as crazy. He died when I was very young, but Mama tells how when boys came to the house to pick up her or my aunt Linda for a date, Granddaddy would harass them just to amuse himself. One of his favorite tactics was to make them nervous by using nonsense words and then acting like they were nuts for not being able to understand him.

"Have you been down to the zizack?" he would ask the boy, who was already worried about impressing Mr. Torans.

"Excuse me, sir?" the boy would say, standing awkwardly in the small front room.

"The *zizack*! The *zizack*! Have you been down to the *zizack*?"

"Uh. . . ," the boy would stammer. "Well . . . yessir, I reckon I have."

Then Granddaddy would bust out laughing until Granny'd catch him and say, "Ellis, you leave that boy alone!"

+ chapter four +

I guess my daddy, Clifton Aubine English, passed the zizack test, because he married my mama in June 1953. When I look at old pictures of them together, I can see that he wasn't always a hard man. In high school, Daddy was a football player, six feet tall and solid, with dark, curly hair. He liked to wear pleated linen pants and a porkpie hat, with the bill cocked off to the side. My mama, Grace, was a cheerleader for another school. In one old black-and-white shot, she's posing with Daddy, him with his quick, bright smile, and her with dark curls bouncing down on her 1940s box-shouldered jacket. Smiling and happy, they were the coolest-looking couple I've ever seen, like movie stars when movie stars were glamorous and perfect.

After they were married, Daddy traveled a lot, selling televisions and other appliances for a company called Hunter Brothers. Later he opened an electronics store and Mama'd go down there and help him run it. But over the years, they grew to despise each other. That's why, for the most part, Mama liked it when Daddy was gone on business. But when he wasn't home, I didn't sleep well. I would lie in bed, eyes wide in the dark, listening to the trailer moan and creak, pecans clacking on the roof, ice trays snapping in the freezer, mice skittering in the walls. Every night, I'd sneak into Biney's room and curl up next to him. I felt better then.

But when Daddy was home, I felt completely safe. I knew he was a tough man who would take care of me. But he was also a loving man, free with hugs, free to say, "I love you." That's what made Aubine English so hard to figure out. Because behind every "I love you" waited a dark flash of anger. Living with Daddy was often like living under a storm cloud. It was almost like there was a charge in the air, like just before a lightning storm. Mama spent a lot of time trying to run interference between me and Daddy, the way she did between me and Daddy's parents. Coming from a house full of laughter, she hated the English family tension.

Mama could make me mad like any other mother, but she never could stand it when I stayed angry. If I was pouting, maybe because she'd told me I couldn't go somewhere, she'd let me stew for a while. But then she'd catch my eye and dance a little jig to try to make me smile. Or maybe, if she was washing dishes, she'd make sure I was watching, then throw one of her legs back like she was kicking herself in the butt. I tried really hard not to laugh, because I was having such a good time pouting. But I couldn't help it. Mama could always get me to giggle.

Sometimes Daddy could be as funny and lighthearted as Mama. As a little boy, I waited and prayed and hoped for those rare bright moments when his smile lit up my world like sunlight. But mostly, I was afraid of his wrath. Daddy says now that the reason he was so strict was because he didn't want Ma English and Daddy Dewey, watching as they did, to catch me doing anything foolish. I wonder now, though, if my grandparents bred a hardness in Daddy that became a brand all its own.

Like Daddy Dewey, Aubine wasn't much of an encourager. For example, Biney and I played Little League and were both pretty good ballplayers. At home Daddy'd take time to play catch with us, bending down on one knee to show me how to grip the laces or how to snap my wrist to get more speed on a pitch. But when Daddy watched us, he would never cheer us on. Instead, every time we swung a bat, he'd yell, "Yer tryin' to kill it!" Even when we'd hit a home run.

Throughout my childhood, Daddy described me to my face with a certain set of adjectives, an alphabet of criticisms: I was "difficult" and "lazy," Daddy said, and "rebellious." I was always trying to be "different," he fumed, which was true, but maybe not any truer for me than for other people who turn out to pursue creative professions. As time passed, when I did succeed at something, I felt like a fake. I felt that at any second someone would pull back the curtain like a skeptic exposing a magic trick and show everybody that I wasn't *really* a good ballplayer or a good singer or even a good person. I was only rebellious, difficult, and lazy, just like Daddy said I was. These criticisms, combined with the whispers that had filtered across the road from Daddy Dewey, began to make me feel that I was destined for failure. It seems crazy that I carried these ideas into my singing career. Even when I began winning Dove awards and walking onstage to accept them, I had this weird sensation that just before handing me the statue, the presenter would reread the paper from the envelope and declare to the audience that he had read my name by mistake.

Of course, neither Daddy nor I knew at the time I would grow up to be a singer. Looking back, I know he did the best he could. And as much as we clashed, I still loved my father and yearned for his attention. Because he traveled, I didn't get to see him much during the week. So I especially loved it when he came to my baseball games. He'd breeze into town from a sales trip and head straight for the ball field.

Daddy went to see Biney play too. Biney was a mean pitcher and could make the ball dance well enough that Art Meyers, a scout from the Detroit Tigers, started coming to watch him play. Mr. Meyers courted Biney with boxloads of big-league-caliber gloves and bats. Two or three times, Mr. Meyers brought him baseballs signed by future Tigers Hall of Famers. Once he even paid for Biney, Daddy, and me to go to Washington, D.C. to watch a major league game.

Every year I burned for baseball season. I loved it, everything about it. The smell of the leather, the crack of the ball hitting the sweet spot on the bat, the red dirt, even the lousy umpires. When spring rolled around, I couldn't wait for the first day of practice. On that day, I'd show up early, but not too early, because I didn't want to look goofy and overeager. But I was. At home on game days, I'd go to the window every hour or so to check for rain clouds. If I saw one, I'd think, *If it's going to rain, it had better do it quick so it'll have time to dry up.* And if a game or even a practice got rained out, I'd actually gripe at God a little. "You could stop this rain if You wanted to!" I'd say and slump down on the couch to mope in front of the TV.

the prodigal comes home

We played ball at a community field right in the middle of Wallace. I thought it was a beautiful place. A brick wall surrounded a combination football field and baseball field with a high backstop and real grandstands for fans. Along the wall, the park managers sold "sponsor" space to national chains like McDonald's and Piggy Wiggly and local businesses like the *Wallace Enterprise*, the hometown paper.

One day when I was about fifteen, Mr. Meyers called Mama and Daddy about me. "I want to come take a look at Mike," he said. "When's he going to be pitching?"

When they told me, I was completely terrified. It was one thing to have Mr. Meyers come and watch Biney. But me? A big league scout watch *me*? For days my stomach felt like the inside of a pan of Jiffy Pop.

The summer day that Mr. Meyers came to watch me pitch was a perfect day for baseball—sunny but not too hot. I put on my Dodgers uniform, which was 1970s sunshine yellow. We were playing the Braves that day, and from the pitching mound, I could see the field entrance off to my right. Every time someone walked in, my stomach popped and jittered. But when I saw it wasn't Mr. Meyers, I'd go back to pitching, half disappointed and half relieved.

Before long, though, Mr. Meyers did come in, and I happened to be on the mound. I started talking to myself frantically. *Okay, Mike: Now's your chance! You can't mess up. If you ever want to be a ballplayer, you have to do good* now!

I faced off a couple of batters. The first one, a lanky kid with zits, grounded out to first. The second batter got a single off me. Then the third batter stepped up to the plate. Mike Melville was a tall, good-looking blond athlete who dated the prettiest girls in school. You know: the kind of guy you want to hate. But he was nice too, so I liked him. A right-hander, Mike squared up to the plate and waggled his bat over his shoulder. He eyeballed me on the mound, looking confident from underneath the visor of his batting helmet.

I eyeballed him right back and tried to forget about the Tigers scout watching me from the stands. Gathering power with a slow, high-kick windup, I threw my nastiest fastball.

And hit Mike Melville squarely in the head.

The crowd gasped. Mike sat down heavily in the dirt and clutched his head for a moment. The umpire squatted to see if he was okay, then stood up, pointed down the right field line, and said the worst words: "Take your base."

Mike was a tough guy. He hiked himself up and trotted to first. My heart sank. I didn't want to look over at Mr. Meyers, but I couldn't help glancing that way; and when I did, he was walking out. It was the last time he ever came to see me play.

That day laid down a pattern for my life. After that, when anything important or special came up, fear gripped me. Fear that I wouldn't be on my game. Fear that I would prove Daddy Dewey right. And after I became a "star," that fear escalated to panic.

+ chapter five +

I have an early record of my "star potential." It's an old 8mm film Daddy made of Biney and me rehearsing a song for church. Biney must have been ten or eleven, and there he is, flickering in black-and-white, out in front of the trailer where the light was better. His hair is parted on the side and slicked over, and I'm beside him, just six or seven years old, squinting at the camera from underneath a buzz cut. We're both wearing dark slacks and white button-up shirts. You can't hear us because Daddy's camera didn't record sound, but you can tell we're singing, because our necks are stretched out a little and our mouths are moving in sync.

As the film rolls, Biney is paying attention and looking into the camera, but my eyes start to wander off. Then I slowly raise my hand and, still singing, poke my finger straight up my nose. Biney looks over and slaps me.

I've sung Southern gospel ever since I can remember. We started out singing as a family and called ourselves what we were: the English Family. The thing you have to understand about Southern gospel is that it is its whole own world. There were groups everywhere. Some were "local" and some were "full-time." Anybody who was serious about singing Southern gospel idolized the full-timers, groups like the Blackwood Brothers, the Inspirations, the Stamps, the Kingsmen, and the Happy Goodman Family. Daddy collected their records, and when he played them, I loved it. So I grew up on Southern gospel—not just in church, but all the time. It was the music of my childhood, and its sweet, soulful harmonies became the sound-track of my life.

Every Sunday morning, while we were getting ready for church, Daddy tuned in to *Jubilee*, the hottest gospel show on television. My family wasn't particularly religious; we mainly went to church because that was what people did. We said grace before meals, and before we went to bed at night Mama always reminded us, "Don't forget to say your prayers."

The English Family—Mama, Daddy, Biney, and me—sang in a few small churches here and there around Wallace. But mostly we sang "specials" at our own little church, North East Pentecostal Free Will Baptist. As far as I know, the denomination exists only in North Carolina, with a handful of out-posts in Virginia and Florida. The Free Will Baptists got their start in New England in the late 1900s. Then, after the Azusa Street Mission revival broke out in Los Angeles, a feud broke out among Free Willers over what the Holy Spirit does and when He does it. It was a fight that lasted until 1959, when the Pentecostal Free Will Baptist movement officially declared itself.

The "Pentecostal" part meant that the Holy Ghost regularly showed up in North East, North Carolina, on Sunday mornings. Lots of "Amens!" during the sermon, spontaneous prayer and healings, that sort of thing. Every once in a while, a brother or sister broke out and spoke in tongues. Not the sort of thing those uptight New England Free Willers would have approved of at all.

But if our church ancestors fought over the Holy Ghost, there was one thing they agreed on: each person personally chooses either to accept or to reject Christ, and because we all choose our salvation, we can also lose it.

That meant you had to follow the rules.

Growing up, I was as afraid of God as of my daddy. I had learned in Sunday school that if I wandered off the straight and narrow—which I took to mean skipping school or cutting up in church—God wouldn't think twice about sending me straight to hell. I didn't see Him as a loving and compas-sionate Creator, Someone who waited for me with open arms. Instead, I thought of God as the Hall Monitor of heaven, stern-faced and just waiting for me to mess up so He could dole out the punishment.

I don't remember exactly how old I was when the North East Free Willers put on a revival week, even calling in visiting preachers to stir things up. On one of those nights, a guest preacher spoke with such force and conviction that I sat still and listened the whole time. At the end of his message, he said, "If anyone feels a tugging at his or her heart right now, that's God asking you to dedicate your life to Him. If you feel a tugging, I want you to come on down to the front right now and confess your sins to Jesus!"

I thought maybe I felt something. Was it God tugging at my heart? Or was it just the pull of peer pressure as I saw other kids, friends of mine, going forward and bowing on their knees? I decided it was God and marched down the aisle and prayed the sinner's prayer. From what I knew about Him, I was afraid not to.

Daddy was the music director at church. And when I was about ten, he started playing bass guitar and managing a gospel quartet that Biney formed with me, his friend Terry Carter, and another Free Will Baptist boy. We called ourselves the Singing Samaritans.

The Singing Samaritans traveled farther than the English Family, through both Carolinas and Virginia, performing in these little bitty churches, maybe seventy-five or a hundred seats, and way off in the country. I was still just ten when we made our first record, *He Pilots My Ship.* Even though we were excited about it, it wasn't as big of a deal as it sounds. Lots of local gospel groups made their own records and sold them after church services on eight-track tapes and crackly-sounding vinyl. Altogether, the Singing Samaritans cut nine records. It wasn't long before Daddy decided we were good enough to go to Nashville and compete at the National Gospel Quartet Convention.

You know how Little League has its World Series and major league baseball has the real World Series? Well, for serious Southern gospel singers, the National Quartet Convention was both of those series rolled into one. J. D. Sumner of the Blackwood Brothers founded the convention in 1957, gathering all the major gospel groups for a three-day concert at the Ellis Auditorium in Memphis. By the mid-1960s, the annual event stretched over a week, drawing more than twenty thousand people.

By the time I came along, the convention had moved to the historic Ryman Auditorium in Nashville. Every year, the Singing Samaritans, four singers plus assorted musicians, piled into the ten-passenger van that Daddy had bought to haul us around in and headed out to Music City, USA. We especially looked forward to the competition that the convention organizers held on Saturday morning where local quartets tried to outsing each other. We saw that as our big chance to break out. If we won, we thought, our chances were better that we could go full-time. If you were full-time, you were making money at it. That was why we went.

Another attraction was the evening concerts, featuring all the gospel greats—the Blackwoods, the Inspirations, the Le Fevres, the Happy Goodmans. As a kid whose parents didn't think much of Elvis, my musical heroes were men like Pat Hoffmaster and J. D. Sumner. Funny thing was, I found out later that they were Elvis's heroes too.

At the National Gospel Quartet Convention, one concert in particular put stars in my eyes. I was sitting with Daddy, Biney, Terry, and some other boys way up toward the back of the Ryman Auditorium, which until 1974 was the home of the Grand Ole Opry. On the bill were the Inspirations, then the Blackwood Brothers. It was 1976, the year that "Learning to Lean" was the number one song. At that time, Pat Hoffmaster sang tenor for the Blackwoods. I loved the Blackwoods as a group, but I thought Pat was in a league of his own.

That night there was this moment, this one moment, when I had a flash of calling, a sense that I knew what I wanted to be in life. The Blackwoods were winding up their set with "Learning to Lean" and, as they say in Southern gospel, were "bringing it home." The bass singer dived down low and hit the bottom note, and Pat's voice soared up to hit the high tenor ending. Then James Blackwood jumped up and nailed Pat's tenor part, and a split second later, Pat's voice sailed even higher and hit the octave. Their voices blended like honey on that last note, and I was completely mesmerized. Think of the thing you love to do the most and imagine watching your hero do it perfectly. I couldn't have been any happier if I'd caught a Babe Ruth home run.

Later, when I was with the Gaither Vocal Band, I met Pat Hoffmaster when we both sang at a Southern gospel awards show. He was getting on in years by then, and a few years after that, he passed away. I'll always regret that I was too shy to tell him about that long-ago night in Nashville when he sang so beautifully that he inspired a little boy to want to be just like him.

+ chapter six +

The Singing Samaritans started singing more and more dates, maybe because we did a lot of things to pattern ourselves after the big gospel groups. For one thing, we all dressed alike—that was the cool thing to do back then—and not just in any old shirts and slacks. Our first matching outfits were classic 1970s tan leisure suits with huge cuffed bell-bottoms, black velvet lapels, and black bow ties. The first time I put mine on, I felt like a million bucks.

Another thing we did to be like the full-time groups was to have an emcee. Every successful group had one member who talked to the audience, made people laugh, and got them hiked up for the next song. The Hensons had their bass singer, Ronnie. The Kingsmen had Jim Hamill. The Singing Samaritans had Terry Carter.

Terry sang baritone for us, and even though he was only a teenager, he was an expert at what is known in Southern gospel as "selling the song." There we'd be, four spit-and-polished country boys onstage in a warm little church, the pews filled with families in their Sunday country best. We'd be singing some up-tempo song like "Living in Canaan," an old-timey number with a camp-meeting beat, and the church would be clapping along. Singing the tenor part, I'd hit that final high note, and Terry would grab the mike off the stand with his left hand and raise his right. "Y'all enjoy that? Y'all like that kind of singing?" he'd ask the congregation, encouraging them with a smile.

the prodigal comes home

They'd burst into applause, ladies nodding and smiling at each other over those cute boys from North East. Then Terry would say, "Let's sing that last verse again!" and we'd launch into the same verse, this time with more soul, more conviction.

In Southern gospel, a lot of groups don't think it's enough just to get onstage, sing, and then sit down. They want the congregation to have a *spiritual experience*. Some of this is genuine. I've seen singers move an audience to tears because of the genuine depth of their feelings for the words they were singing. But I have seen many more use proven techniques, adding a dose of drama to milk all the right emotions, to get an audience to cry. I have done both myself – because I was taught to. I whimpered through a verse, prayed aloud between verses, and "walked the footlights" while I sang. Sometimes I stopped singing altogether to share a moving story, many times bringing little old ladies to tears.

You see, crying congregations buy more records. And gospel quartets almost always have records to sell after the show. I grew up being taught that making people cry or get up out of the pews and clap and carry on was just part of the business. And after the Singing Samaritans had been together for a while, I got in trouble if I didn't participate.

When we first started singing together, we'd be onstage somewhere, and I'd just stand there and sing. It wasn't too long, though, before Daddy started pulling me aside after the shows. "You need to *do* more," he'd say. "Walk a little. *Testify.*" And if I talked back to him and told him I didn't want to, he'd slap my face.

Once while singing during a recording session with the Singing Samaritans, the lyrics and the message of the song moved me to tears so that I struggled to finish. I thought Daddy'd be mad that I messed up the session. Instead, he grinned. "We'll leave that on there," he said, gloating a little. "That's gonna be great!"

The thing was, he knew it would sell. And it did.

The contradictions ate away at me. I loved to sing but hated to act. I genuinely felt the emotions of the songs, but I hated being made to go through certain motions. I especially hated it when Daddy decided that I was old enough to "give my testimony." Biney started testifying when he was about sixteen, and I knew my turn was next. I was shy but also pretty tough, a serious ballplayer and all that. I hated the thought of all those little old ladies patting me on the head afterward and telling me how cute I was. Worse than that, though, the thought of getting up in front of folks and talking about the wonderful things the Lord had done in my life terrified me. I was only about twelve or thirteen years old; as far as I knew, He hadn't done much yet.

When my time finally ran out and Daddy made me testify, I just mumbled something I'd heard him say. As odd as it sounds for someone who would go on to sing for a living, I was very, very shy. Later my shyness would threaten my success with the Gaithers. Back then, though, Daddy just thought I was being a rebel. It got to where at every concert, when Terry was bringing it home and the crowd was clapping and singing along, my dad would lower his brow and give me a look that said, "*Say* something. *Do* something—or you're going to get it."

And if I didn't, I did.

Daddy slapped me in the face a lot. He slapped me when we were alone. Worse, he slapped me in front of other people. He was very quick with his hands, like a fast gun. *Pow!*—and my face was swelling up. If he had been a gunfighter, he could have killed them all. Once, we sang at a little church off in the country somewhere, and after we sang, the preacher gave a message. Instead of staying and listening, Biney, Terry Carter, and I walked to the little store across the street from the church to get a Coke and a candy bar. We knew we were taking a chance. And sure enough, when we crossed the street again, there was Daddy, waiting at the top of the church steps, his mouth just a slash in his face. When I saw him, my stomach dropped to my knees. As we three boys walked slowly up the steps, I got ready because I knew what was coming.

Bam! Bam! Biney and I both got it in the face. Terry Carter told me later he thought he was going to be next. He still tells about the day he barely missed getting slapped by Aubine English.

As THE SINGING SAMARITANS booked more and more dates, I became torn between gospel music and baseball. I knew there was no way to commit to both, because baseball demanded all my spare time and so did singing. During my last year of Little League, my team won the league championship and I was selected for the All-Star team. I also won several awards, including two really big ones: the home run trophy (I set the league record for most homers) and Most Valuable Player. I was thirteen years old, and I couldn't wait to go to my first really big awards ceremony. I imagined how proud Mama and Daddy would be when I walked up to accept those trophies.

But it turned out that Daddy had booked a concert for the same night. I begged him to let me skip it, but he dug in like he always did and refused. "We've booked a date, and we're going to keep it," he said. "We have a responsibility."

I didn't care about responsibility. I cared about being a kid winning baseball trophies. But I didn't dare disobey Daddy, so I went to the concert, which turned out to be in a little Podunk church with a congregation of about fifty people. That night when we got home, I walked into the dark trailer. There, sitting on the coffee table, were more trophies than I'd ever seen. Mama had gone to the ceremony and accepted them for me. I should have been excited to win them all. Instead, all I felt was disappointment. It was my last year of Little League, and I had won every award there was to win, top dog for a day. I felt bitter at having missed what I thought was one of the most important nights of my life.

It was a defining moment in my relationship with Daddy. For my whole life, he'd reinforced the message that I wouldn't amount to anything. When I finally did, he ignored it. Maybe that's why I didn't tell him what happened in the back of the van on the way home that night, as it had so many nights before.

+ chapter seven +

I don't remember exactly when it started or ended, but I was very young when one of the older boys in the Singing Samaritans started touching me in places he shouldn't have. I won't tell his name here—through the years, we had at least a dozen musicians and singers rotate through the group—but I'll call him Ed.

Ed was older, sixteen or seventeen. Over six feet tall, he leaned a little past heavy, had a big head, and wore his wiry brown hair parted on the side. Ed wore thick glasses and had a high-pitched speaking voice that seemed weird coming out of someone his size. He wasn't effeminate, but he wasn't a jock. He was more like . . . an accountant. I especially remember his hands. He had big hands. They were warm and moist, with the nails bitten down. Even today, when I see someone with hands like his, my stomach churns.

After our concerts, the Singing Samaritans would pile into the van and begin the long drive home. It was always nighttime, and we'd hum over the highways through the dark, usually for about two or three hours. I was still small enough to where if I wanted to sleep, I could curl up on the floor of the van. Ed always maneuvered the seating so that he could sleep on the seat above me. I didn't think anything of it, until one night when I felt a hand touch my body.

Ed started rubbing my back, which I thought was a little strange, but not so strange that I would call attention to it. After all, I was lying on the floor right behind the driver's seat where Daddy was. I was safe, wasn't I?

Then Ed's hand moved slowly down until he was rubbing my backside. Creeping fear spread through my belly, but I didn't know what to do. So I pretended to be asleep. Ed kept rubbing and rubbing. Then he started pulling on my hip, trying to get me to turn over. I wanted to scream, "Daddy! Daddy!" But I was afraid that if I said anything, Ed would just lie and say he had been asleep, that his hand had fallen off the seat above me and accidentally brushed me. Daddy was always blaming me for things. Ed was a church-going teenager, singing for the Lord in a gospel group. Why would Daddy believe me over him?

So I kept on playing possum, and Ed kept on molesting me. He snaked his warm, nasty hand along my backside and between my legs on almost every trip for two years. It disgusted me, but I became especially disgusted with myself. I thought something was wrong with me and wrestled with self-hatred in my mind: *You must like it, 'cause if you didn't, you'd tell somebody and make him quit. But if I tell somebody,* I argued with myself, *Daddy'll find out, and that would break up the Singing Samaritans, and he'd be mad, and it would be my fault.*

By then Ed was nearly a grown-up, and it would be my word against a grown-up's word. He could lie and say he never touched me. Who was going to believe me?

Finally, Ed announced he was leaving the group. *I'm free!* I thought, relieved that I didn't have to deal anymore with the choice of submitting and feeling dirty or telling and risking my father's anger. That was the end of it for years, until one day I told my mother.

She gave me a long hug and said, "That explains why you'd hide in your room and ask me to tell him you weren't home every time he came over to the house."

Finally, I told Daddy. He said, "No wonder you were so rebellious as a boy."

I thought that was that—that I'd been right not to tell him sooner. But the next day, Daddy called me and said he couldn't get Ed off his mind. He was sick about it and wished he'd known. Years later I found out that Ed had molested other neighborhood kids for a long time and had even tried messing with other members of the Singing Samaritans. I also learned that he had gone on to become a grade school teacher.

+ chapter eight +

Ed and his night moves weren't the only secrets I kept during those years. The other secret was that my mama drank. I don't know how else to say it. I used to see Mama and Daddy both drinking at family parties when I was real little, but I didn't know it was a problem until one night when I was about seven years old. We'd already moved to North East and were living in Ma English and Daddy Dewey's house. It was dark outside, bedtime, and Biney and I slept in the same room. We were already in there, getting ready for bed, but I could feel an anxiousness running through the house like live electricity. It was always that way, like the low-grade hum of high-tension wires.

I had already pulled off my clothes and put on pajamas when I heard Daddy holler, "Biney, Mike, come here!"

When I heard the tone of his voice, a layer of dread settled into my belly. Biney and I looked at each other with a familiar mix of worry and resignation. We knew that tone by now. Biney opened the bedroom door, and I followed him through it, hiding in his larger shadow. We crossed the hall into the kitchen on bare feet.

I saw Daddy standing by the sink. Mama stood next to him, her head hanging down like a whipped puppy.

"Come here, boys. I want you to see somethin'," Daddy said. In his hand he held a glass half full of a clear liquid that looked like water. He thrust it toward us. "Smell it."

the prodigal comes home

I was afraid not to obey Daddy, so I followed Biney over, and we each sniffed the glass, both wincing at the oily tang of vodka. I hated smelling that glass. Even though I was only a small boy, I knew I was being forced to take sides against my mama. Tears welled up in my eyes and spilled over. Biney set his jaw and looked down at the cracked white linoleum.

"See what your Mama's doin' to us?" Daddy said as he upended the glass over the sink. I heard the vodka splash down, then gurgle into the drain. "Go on, now," Daddy said.

Even though I was afraid to, I stole a glance at Mama. I was desperate to catch her eye, to let her know that I still loved her even if Daddy didn't. But she didn't look at me. Mama kept her chin down on her chest, her hair hanging around her face like a curtain.

As we walked back to our room, I thought I could feel Daddy's eyes burning into my back. I felt so sorry for Mama, for Daddy humiliating her that way in front of us. When Biney shut the door behind us, I began to sob, but silently, afraid Daddy would hear me. He couldn't have heard me, though. They were yelling so loudly at each other that the house seemed to tremble as we crawled into bed. My tears poured and my throat seemed so tight that it felt like I couldn't breathe.

Biney just held me. "Everything's going to be all right," he said.

But it wasn't. When you're the child of a drinker, memories of childhood don't unreel like a movie, where you can see that the really bad times were surrounded by plenty of better ones. Instead, childhood often flashes through your mind like some kind of dark slide show organized by a demon.

There are two slides I wish I could burn. One involved a hairbrush; the other involved an ax.

The hairbrush incident happened about a year after Daddy poured Mama's drink down the drain. It hurts to think about it, because I loved Mama so much, and one thing I especially loved was her long black hair. It was as dark as a raven's wings, and I loved to brush it. One night I was watching TV in the living room and Mama plopped down on the floor and waved me over with a loose flip of her wrist. "Come on over here, baby, and brush Mama's hair," she slurred.

I stood slowly and looked at her. Her eyes were loose and lazy. She tried to put on a bright, alert look, but her head lolled just a little bit too far to the right and her smile was slack and shaped wrong. You could tell the difference between Mama drinking and Mama not. By then I lived with a dread in my stomach that washed in and out like a tide. It was high tide now as I took the brush from her hand and sat behind her. She reeked of liquor—not vodka, but something dark like the whiskey I'd smelled at parties.

I hated that when she smelled that way, she didn't act like my mama. She was a different person. "That feels good," she said, her head falling back farther and farther with each brushstroke. "You love your mama, don't you?"

I did love her. That's why my heart was breaking.

I despised her liquor. What it did to her. How it took my beautiful raven-haired, green-eyed mother and turned her dull and slurry. How liquor lured her to stay home from my concerts and Little League games to keep company with it instead.

By the time I was in fifth and sixth grade, I was angry—not at Mama, but at the liquor itself. I had no sense at all that she was to blame, that she could choose to drink or not to drink. So I blamed the bottles and made it my mission to eliminate my enemies. Three or four days a week, the house was empty when I got home from school. Mama was either running errands or helping my brother down at the store. On those days, I checked the house for liquor bottles. I almost always found some hiding in the vanity cabinet under the sink in Mama's bathroom.

I didn't really want to look for them, but it seemed like I couldn't help it. Their existence was a shameful secret, something that made me different. I was sure other kids didn't live with a secret stash of liquor under the bathroom sink. When I came home to an empty house, the vanity cabinet both drew me and repelled me. Checking Mama's supply was the first thing I did after school. I'd walk quietly back to her bedroom, my stomach light and scared, like on the trip to the highest point on a roller coaster. I *had* to look, but I didn't want to find. I almost always did, though: one or two bottles, pints or fifths, dark or clear, sometimes both. Working quickly, afraid I'd hear the door open and footsteps any second, I'd unscrew the caps and pour the poison down the sink. I hated the smells, the subtle tang of vodka, bourbon's oaky sweetness. I poured out as much as I dared, hoping Mama would think she drank it.

the prodigal comes home

THAT WENT ON FOR YEARS, until one day, when I was about thirteen, I had had enough. I remember that it was a gray day, cool but not cold. After school I walked up the dirt driveway and around back, looking across the chipped-paint fence at the empty dirt fields beyond. The tobacco had long since been harvested, and the fields seemed bleak and lonely.

Drawn curtains covered the louvered window on the back door of the trailer. The door was unlocked, and I stepped inside.

"Mama?" I called like I always did.

No answer. I pulled the door shut behind me and turned right, heading down the narrow hallway to Mama's bathroom. I opened the vanity cabinet door, hoping not to find anything. That happened every once in a while. But instead of only one bottle, or even two, I found four.

Somewhere inside my mind, a fuse blew. My skin flushed hot, and I know that if I had looked in the vanity mirror, my face would have glowed red with rage. I snatched up the bottles by their necks, two in each hand. Their sides clashed together dangerously, but I didn't care. I stomped back up the hall, bent to twist the doorknob, kicked the door open, jumped to the ground, and kicked it shut again.

My fury, at first, turned me methodical, all business, like a parent without remorse avenging a wounded child. There was a little outbuilding on the property, white paint peeling off, sitting next to a pecan tree. I made a straight line there, passed two bottles from my right hand into the crook of my left arm, reached inside, and grabbed an ax. I stalked to the back fence and pitched the bottles through it one by one onto the fallow ground on the other side, then heaved the ax through. I climbed over, picked up the bottles and my weapon, and marched out into the field.

Thirty, forty, fifty yards, I carried the bottles and the ax. I don't know why I stopped where I did. But suddenly I dropped the bottles, hoisted the ax high, and brought it down hard, smashing the glass.

Liquor splashed up, then mingled dark with clear and soaked the dirt. Over and over, I raised the ax blade and brought it down on the glass. The breaking was music, and the crunch of the glass sounded like victory. Righteous anger fired my arms so that I felt I could have smashed granite. I aimed my fury at those bottles because *I loved my mother* and those bottles were taking her away from me. It only took moments, though, for my rage to melt into grief. Hot tears squirted from my eyes and streamed down my cheeks. Again and again I brought down the ax, sobs breaking free as I crushed the bottles to nothing.

I don't know how much time passed before the big ax became heavy. Finally, I stopped and let it hang at my side. Exhausted and out of breath, I realized I had been acting like a maniac in the middle of an open field. I spun around and looked anxiously at the back door of the trailer—just in time to see the curtain over the louvered windows slip from open to closed.

It had to be Mama. Nobody else was ever home at that hour.

At first I was terrified. All this time, when I'd come home and emptied those bottles, nothing was ever said about it. I was never detected. My stomach quivered: *She's caught me.* This was the big one. Not just me pouring them down the drain.

I didn't go straight back to the house. Quietly, I walked back to the outbuilding and put away the ax. Then I grabbed the basketball and started shooting hoops into the old, makeshift goal that stood under the pecan tree. Anything to keep from having to go back in the house. Mama and I never talked about that day, but she quit drinking. Years later she told me how: she got on her knees and prayed that she would never take another drink. "I prayed to God that if I did, He'd make me sicker than a dog."

She never told me when she prayed that prayer. But after that day in the tobacco field, I never found more liquor bottles. And Mama became my mama again.

+ chapter nine +

In school I was an average student, mainly because whenever teachers assigned books to read, I found myself unable to concentrate for more than a few minutes at a time. I'd begin reading at the top of a page and get to the bottom without knowing what I'd read. It's not that I had trouble with the words or comprehension or anything like that. It was just that I could plan my breakfast, lunch, and dinner menu, figure out what I was going to do that weekend, make a mental note to call Mama, and never stop reading. I've never been diagnosed with attention deficit disorder or a learning disability. But it was that way for as long as I can remember.

This carried over to reading the Bible. It wasn't that I didn't want to learn what God had to say in His Word; it was that every time I started reading, my mind wandered—and not just while reading Leviticus. And since I was onstage from the time I was a little boy, ministering to people, I was too embarrassed to say, "Hey, I'm having trouble studying the Bible." I felt like I was supposed to know it all already. It seemed like everyone around me did.

I wish I had told someone, because I needed the pure milk of the Word to nourish and sustain me. Instead, what I got was a different preacher almost every week. Like I said before, the Singing Samaritans were performing all over three states. And with very few exceptions, I never stopped traveling. Sunday to Sunday, church to church—a fire-breathing, hell-and-damnation country preacher one week, a theological egghead the next. Was I eternally saved or hanging by a thread over Hades? Was I saved by grace or damned by works? Was I going home to glory in the rapture or witnessing Christ during the Battle of Armageddon? I didn't know. So I just mouthed what I thought were the right words and kept on singing.

I graduated from high school in 1980 without much idea of what I was going to do with my life. By then Biney worked at the world-famous Barcalounger recliner plant in Turkey, North Carolina, and he got me a job there. I didn't last long. I started on a Wednesday lifting recliners onto a conveyor belt. By the next Wednesday morning, I was on another part of the line, making boxes to fit over the Barcaloungers. Over and over, all morning long, I bent and stapled heavy-gauge cardboard into empty containers, each one big enough to bury a fat man. The work was so boring I wanted to scream, and after a while, I started thinking, *I've got to sing or play ball or do* something, *because I sure as heck ain't doing* this *all my life.* By lunchtime, I quit and went to go see Granny. She always seemed to have the right thing to say.

"What you wanna do with your life, baby?" Granny asked, spooning some of her homemade grape jelly onto some of her miraculous biscuits.

"Sing," I said, "or play baseball."

But there didn't seem to be too many ways to earn money doing either one of those, we agreed. Especially since I'd nailed Mike Melville in the head and the Singing Samaritans seemed to be winding down. We were singing fewer dates and seemed to have lost our momentum.

"What about cutting hair?" I said, thinking of Daddy Dewey.

"Well, it's in your family," Granny said. "You ought to think about doing that."

That's how I wound up in cosmetology school in Wilmington, North Carolina, population 7,500. It seemed like the big city to me, sophisticated in its lack of tobacco fields and chickens. At cosmetology school, I learned how to cut and style and perm and blow dry—enough to do Mama and Aunt Linda's hair for years afterward. But only as a treat, because I hadn't been in school but a few months when I got a call from a man named Jerry Hatley.

Years before, Jerry had played piano so well for the Singing Samaritans that a full-time group called the Singing Americans had spotted him at the quartet convention and offered him a job. Now they needed a new singer, and Jerry asked me if I wanted to try out. The offer sent my mind spinning off in new directions. I'd always thought that if I ever made it in music, it would be with my family. Plus, I'd always sung tenor, never lead. But I remembered the first thing I told Granny when she asked me what I was interested in: singing. So I told Jerry yes, got in my car, and drove to Maiden, North Carolina, to audition.

I got the job. Then I went home at Christmas and told my family I was quitting cosmetology school to sing full-time. Predictably, Daddy shut down like a vault. Wouldn't even speak to me. Biney was angry too. Without them saying a word, I knew they saw my decision as rebellion, as a sign that I couldn't stick with anything I started—not a simple trade school, not even a job making boxes. I felt cornered, beaten. I wanted to sing—to earn a living doing something I loved, something I was good at. But Daddy made me feel so bad that I called Charlie Burke, the man who owned the Singing Americans, and told him I wasn't going to be able to join the group.

"But we've got a date booked this weekend, and we don't have anybody else to sing lead," Charlie said. "Can you just fill in until we find somebody?"

I told him I could do that much. It was a decision that would change my life.

The next weekend, in January 1981, I sang lead with the Singing Americans at a concert in Charleston, West Virginia. We performed in a downtown auditorium, and while I was onstage, I had this moment of clarity, of *rightness*. It was as though I had always been looking at my future through a telescope that was slightly out of focus, but that night God suddenly turned the lens and made the picture clear. Instantly, I knew that what I wanted to do was also what God wanted me to do, what He had gifted me to do.

During intermission, I ran backstage and called my mother from a pay phone. "Mama, I'm staying with the group. I know this is what I'm supposed to do," I said. "I'm not coming home."

She was quiet for a moment. Then she said, "Doll-baby, I knew you weren't. I knew that once you got out there, you wouldn't ever come back."

+ chapter ten +

Charlie Burke, the owner of the Singing Americans, also owned a bus company, a fish camp, and a funeral home. He was a tough man who'd squeeze a nickel until it screamed; I sometimes thought his heart must be made of rawhide. We rehearsed in a room in the funeral home not far from where dead men lay, pancaked and rouged, wearing suits with false pockets and slits up the back. In fact, Charlie made the Singing Americans wear dark suits that he was able to get cheap from a company that supplied undertakers. He paid me $125 a week and griped about my mustache, the kind of clothes I wore offstage, and the length of my hair. Once Charlie even held my wages until I went and got it cut. But I put up with it because I was finally *full-time*. I was nineteen years old and getting paid to sing.

Plus, I loved the other guys in the group, especially Ed Hill, a Southern gospel legend who'd been with the Kingsmen and the Stamps. In 1924 a hard-charging singer-salesman named Virgil O. Stamps had started a little music company in Texas and from there had built an empire that spun off a string of successful quartets. So Ed came from a fine gospel tradition. And when the Stamps backed Elvis in Vegas, it was Ed whose job it was to say the words that have now become famous: "Ladies and gentleman, Elvis has left the building. Good night and God bless you."

The Singing Americans toured the South, singing in churches and auditoriums and cutting records. I was on the road so much that I didn't even have an apartment of my own. While we traveled, I slept on the tour bus. In between gigs, I stayed with friends and kept my few belongings in my first car, a black Rally Sport Camaro with a clothes rod hanging across the backseat. The group was doing well and had built a fan base even before I joined. And it was through two of those fans that I met the girl who would become my wife.

In the spring of 1981, we were playing Charleston, West Virginia, again, this time for four nights. Tammy and Wendy, both loyal Singing Americans fans, lived in nearby Dunbar and came to hear us. They caught me after a show.

"You've *got* to meet our friend Lisa," Tammy said, describing a slim, blue-eyed blond. "You two would really hit it off."

"Well, bring her tomorrow night," I said. "I'd like to meet her."

Tammy and Wendy said they would. But the next night, when they showed up, Lisa wasn't with them. "We tried to get her to come," Wendy said, "but she said she had some other things she was doing."

This intrigued me, of course. I liked the fact that she hadn't come running down to meet me. Also, Tammy and Wendy kept telling me how beautiful their friend was, with a big smile and a bubbly personality.

"You'll just love her!" they said.

"Well, get her here!" I said.

"We're trying!"

On our last night in Charleston, we were booked to sing at a church. Things were pretty informal then—we didn't wait backstage to be introduced, but instead sat out in the sanctuary. The guys and I walked in and sat down on the first row right in front of Tammy and Wendy. And when I turned around to say hi, there sat the most beautiful girl I had ever seen. It sounds cliché, but that's the truth. And when she smiled, that's all it took: I was hooked.

The rest of the night was just fun. I was young and still shy during performances. But with a beautiful girl to impress, I cut loose and showed off a little, every once in a while catching her eye from the stage. After the show, the guys and I went out to the record table to sign autographs. There wasn't much I could do at that point about spending more time with Lisa. Business is business, and we had records to sell. All I could do was watch her from across the room and wish. And before I knew it, our driver had herded us all onto the bus and was revving up the engine and getting ready to roll out of town. Meanwhile, in the same parking lot, Tammy, Wendy, and Lisa had piled into Tammy's car and were also getting ready to leave.

I squirmed in my seat, a little bit frantic. Here I had just met the girl of my dreams, and I didn't know where she lived or how to get in touch with her again. Then the bus started to roll.

"Stop!" I yelled. "Stop the bus for a second!"

I rushed to the front and begged the driver to let me out. "It'll be just a second; I promise."

I jumped out of the bus and ran over to Tammy's car, circling to where Lisa sat in the front passenger seat. She rolled down the window, her face a question mark.

I swallowed hard and said, "I'm sorry, but I fell in love this weekend and I need to get your number."

I know it was corny, but the girls all laughed, and Lisa jotted her number on a piece of paper. I folded it up and tucked it in the pocket of my undertaker suit. Then I ran back to the bus before the driver could take off without me.

Lisa and I began writing letters back and forth between Virginia and North Carolina. She was seventeen and a senior in high school, a great student who excelled on the track team. I was a nineteen-year-old singer living out of my car. I couldn't afford long-distance calls but would save all my quarters so that every once in a while I could plug them into a pay phone and actually talk to her.

After a couple of months, whenever I had some time off, I'd drive down to Dunbar and stay a few days. Lisa and I would go to the movies in Charleston, play video games, hold hands. I hit it off with her parents. They weren't churchgoing people, but Lisa was. She lived across the street from Tammy and hitched a ride to church with her every Sunday morning and night. Which says a lot about Lisa Bailey.

Our courtship went on like that for several months. We talked about getting married—and on one trip, we went to a jewelry store and she showed me which ring she liked. A couple of months later, I secretly went back and bought it. And in 1981, at Christmastime, I asked her to marry me.

+ chapter eleven +

The Singing Americans were doing pretty well, several notches above local groups, but not quite the big time. We made the rounds of the gospel circuit, and I kept going to see Lisa between trips. Charlie Burke got us on the ticket with marquee groups like the Kingsmen and the Hinsons. So by then I was fairly used to meeting and being around a lot of the folks whose music I'd grown up singing and a few who had headlined the evening concerts at the quartet convention. But when Charlie told us he'd booked us on the ticket with the Goodmans at a concert in Winston-Salem, North Carolina, I nearly fainted.

I think most kids in those days had a singer or a group that was *theirs*. Dylan, Willie, Elvis, the Stones, or someone else. It might sound weird to modern ears, but my group growing up was the Happy Goodman Family. The Goodmans had come from a poverty-stricken area on the outskirts of Birmingham, Alabama, to become some of the most famous faces in Southern gospel. As a child, I remember watching them on Jim and Tammy Faye Bakker's *PTL* program on TV.

Now remember: the 1970s was the decade of the rock concert. By the time I was fourteen years old, teenagers across the country were piling into airbrushed conversion vans and driving to the nearest midsized city to hear Lynyrd Skynyrd or ZZ Top. So it might sound weird when I say that I was piling into Daddy's old, boat-length Lincoln Continental to go hear the

the prodigal comes home

Happy Goodmans. I had never traveled just to see a concert before. But as soon as my idols booked a date at the Keenan Auditorium in Wilmington, about an hour from home, I *begged* Daddy to take us. When he said he would, I counted down the days like we were having Christmas twice that year.

Daddy, Biney, Terry, and I made the trip together. Except for the evening performances at the quartet convention in Nashville, the venue was the nicest I'd seen. The Keenan was an *auditorium*, with actual acoustics, not a sports arena or a gym like we were used to. I can't remember for sure how this happened, but we got there early and got seats on the front row. For me, being that close to the Happy Goodmans was like having seats behind home plate at Yankee Stadium.

The group always opened the show the same way, and it was pure magic. Howard Goodman came out and sang a song alone, with piano legend Eddie Crook. Then Howard called his brothers, Rusty and Sam, and they blended their voices: Howard singing lead, Sam tenor, and Rusty baritone. But Howard's wife, Vestal Goodman, wasn't out there yet. That's because Sister Vestal always *made an entrance*.

It was the coolest thing, because she wore this big United Pentecostal hairdo and these sequined dresses that sparkled in the spotlights. And she *never* appeared onstage without her trademark handkerchief in one hand. If I had known that night that someday I would know Vestal as a friend, and that she'd sign one of those hankies and give it to me, framed, as a gift, I would have died then and been happy.

Here's the way Vestal made her entrance that night at the Keenan. The band started playing the first bars of a Goodman signature song, "What a Lovely Name." I can hear it now—the churchy piano chords, the soulful slide of the steel guitar. Then Rusty, Sam, and Howard joined together on the first verse and the chorus:

What a lovely name, this name of Jesus.
Reaching higher far, than the brightest star.
Sweeter than the songs they sing in heaven.
Let the world proclaim, what a lovely name.

The air in the auditorium was electric, because every Goodmans fan in the sold-out house knew what was coming next: Vestal. Sure enough, the band stepped one key higher, and here came Sister Vestal out from behind the curtain like the star that she was, lifting up the next verse with her amazing soprano:

He'll return in clouds of glory.
Saints of ev'ry race shall behold His face.
With Him enter heaven's city,
Ever to proclaim, what a lovely name.

The crowd went crazy, and I went crazy with them, just acted like a complete fool. I laughed out loud with joy, jumped to my feet, and didn't stop grinning for the next hour and a half. This to me was *it*—there's just no other way to explain it. Years later when I met Vestal and heard her singing right next to me, I felt the exact same way—and continued to every time I heard her sing. She had a special stage presence, the power to hold an audience. As I began to work my way up in gospel music, I patterned myself after Vestal Goodman. Well . . . except for the hairdo and the sequined dress.

BY THE TIME CHARLIE BURKE booked the Singing Americans on a ticket with the Goodmans, Vestal and Howard had broken off from the main group, who renamed themselves just "the Goodmans," dropping "Happy" since that was Howard's nickname. Still, for me, meeting Rusty and Sam and singing on the same stage was like coming full circle and was as good as it could get. At least that's what I thought until after the concert.

Granny, Mama, and Aunt Linda had driven over to hear me sing that night. After the show, we were all standing backstage talking when I felt a tap on my shoulder.

"Mike?" It was Rusty Goodman. Just to hear this hero of mine say my name in that great big voice of his was the craziest thing.

"Hi, Rusty," I said, astonished that he even knew who I was. I felt like the little kid in the Coke commercial talking to football great Mean Joe Green.

the prodigal comes home

And here's something else crazy: I'm six foot four, and he was five foot some-thing. But at the time it never even crossed my mind that I had to look way down to have a conversation with him, because to me Rusty Goodman was larger than life.

Well, he made a little small talk at first and was very gracious to Mama and the others. But the only thing I remember for sure was what he said to me when the small talk was through: "Would you be interested in joining the Goodmans?"

I can't remember my answer exactly, but the way I tell it onstage today is that I said to Rusty, "Well-I'm-going-to-have-to-pray-about-it-Yes!"

In the world of Southern gospel, being asked to join the Goodmans wasn't just like getting called up to the majors from the farm team. It was like getting called up to the 1927 Yankees. I was already prayed up on that one. I enjoyed going to tell Charlie Burke I was leaving. His military ways rubbed me the wrong way. Within a week, I had moved to Madisonville, Kentucky, and started rehearsing with Rusty and Sam, along with tenor Johnny Cook, who had once sung with the Florida Boys, an old-school quartet. Tanya Goodman, Rusty's daughter, added a soprano part to the group. We rehearsed in Rusty's basement. Even though the Goodmans were a gospel institution, there wasn't anything special about that basement. There was just a lot of room down there, and Rusty's dear wife, Billie, could close off the racket from upstairs.

I'll never forget the night I debuted with the Goodmans. In fact, I'll never forget the first note we sang onstage together. We had arrived at the venue early enough to rehearse, just the five of us onstage, standing around an upright piano. But when we took our places that night, a five-piece band was behind us, including piano legend Eddie Crook, who had been with the Happy Goodmans when I saw them in Wilmington and long before that. I'd never sung with a band that big.

Our first song in Greensboro that night was "I Believe He's Coming Back Like He Said." When the band counted down and broke into their signature introduction, it was the biggest sound I'd ever heard. Next, I had to open my mouth and sing when what I really wanted to do was stand there and listen, just soak in the moment, and hear those four world-class singers perform.

But I sang, harmonizing with my heroes on a song I'd been hearing them sing for as long as I could remember. At that moment, I felt like I'd arrived. And for maybe the first time in my life, the words "He'll never amount to anything" meant nothing to me.

+ chapter twelve +

I had been with the Goodmans for only a couple of months when two things happened: Lisa and I got married, and the Goodmans headed to Word Music, our Nashville label, to start looking for songs for a new record.

The group was on the hook to produce a new album at the very same time our wedding was scheduled. So after a little church wedding near Lisa's home, she and I drove to Nashville. And to make up for the calendar conflict between our honeymoon and the new record, the Goodmans paid for us to stay at the Maxwell House, a plush hotel near the studio. The truth was, we couldn't have afforded a honeymoon anyway, so we did right well staying at the Maxwell for a whole week. We honeymooned just fine between recording sessions, and Lisa never complained once.

In the music industry, groups that don't write their own material have what are called "song selection meetings." These are highly sophisticated sessions where the people in the group sit around, listen to song after song, and make very technical judgments, such as "I like that one" or "That's awful."

Okay, it's not that simple. But sometimes it seems close. You'll see what I mean in a minute. Singers do have to know what makes a great gospel song. First and above all, the song has to deliver a timeless message about God. Second, a great gospel song should have a soaring, memorable chorus. Third, it should have a great "hook," some catchy lines that get stuck in people's heads.

the prodigal comes home

At the Goodmans' song selection meeting at Word Records, we met with producer Joe Huffman and Lari Goss, a keyboardist known for his brilliant orchestration who is still influential in CCM. Lari and I hit it off, and I still work with him on various projects today.

During that first meeting, which took place in a room that was basically empty except for a piano and a cassette recorder, Rusty said to me, "Mike, you need your own song."

What he meant was that he thought I needed what we call in Southern gospel a "signature song." Lots of rock and contemporary artists are known for their megahits, Johnny Cash, "Walk the Line"; Aretha Franklin, "Respect"; Lynyrd Skynyrd, "Free Bird." But a hit is not the same as a signature song. A song can be a signature song whether or not it sells a bunch of records. It is a song that one artist has claimed as his or her anthem, whose arrangement is considered *the* arrangement, a song people will always associate with *that* artist.

"I've got a song that I think is going to be a really big one for you," Rusty told me.

Now remember, I hadn't been up from the bush leagues for more than a couple of months. The thought of being known for a song of my own was almost too much to imagine. I couldn't wait to hear the song Rusty thought might be the one. He popped a cassette into the machine and pushed play. A mixed group of women and men began to sing a slow, sort of old-fashioned number called "I Bowed on My Knees (and Cried Holy)."

> *I dreamed of a city called Glory.*
> *It was so bright and so fair.*
> *When I entered the gates, I cried "Holy!"*
> *The angels all met me there.*

Rusty let the song play to the end and then called a break. We all agreed to talk about it after we got back. Lari and I stepped outside for a breath of fresh air.

"So what'd you think of the song?" Lari asked me when we were alone.

I'd been hearing about Lari Goss as long as I could remember. He'd been a successful singer and producer for longer than I'd been alive. "What do *you* think?" I asked.

"To tell you the truth," he said in his slow country drawl, "I really don't care for it all that much."

I was so relieved. "Man, I'm glad you said that, because I don't really like it either."

"Well, you need to tell Rusty," Lari said.

"Well, you need to go in and *help* me tell him. I'm new to this thing. I don't want to blow it."

"Well, this is *your* song. You're the one that needs to be happy with it."

I thought a minute, then took a deep breath and let it out. "Okay, I'm gonna tell him, then. I don't want to be singing a song I don't feel comfortable with, so I'm just gonna go in there and tell him."

"Good," Lari assured me. "That's what you need to do."

As we walked back in, I silently rehearsed how I was going to tell Rusty Goodman, a man with decades of experience picking great songs, that I didn't like the one he'd picked for me. I was nervous about it, but I didn't want to get stuck with a dud. We all gathered around the piano again.

Rusty looked at me and got right to the point: "So what do you think of 'I Bowed on My Knees?'"

"I love it!" I said. "Let's do it!"

+ chapter thirteen +

It was a good thing I was such a wimp. I have two or three signature songs today, but "I Bowed on My Knees" was my first number one song and the song people still identify me with today. That didn't happen with the Goodmans, though, because just a couple of months after we cut the record, the group broke up. I was devastated. I called home, and Daddy was nice enough to drive out to Kentucky, collect Lisa and me, and drive us back to North Carolina.

Already Lisa and I had begun to fight on a regular basis. She thought I was lazy around the house. I thought she nagged too much. She thought I spent too much money and always had to have the best. I thought she was a penny pincher. We went around and around, yelling at each other, young and unable to communicate, with no skills to work things out.

Add to that the fact that I was now unemployed and back in Wallace, a musical flash in the pan. Lisa and I moved into the double-wide with Mama and Daddy for three months, then found an apartment to rent. I went back to singing in churches with Daddy and Biney, although we didn't get paid. Sometimes congregations took up a small offering and we shared that. As far as I was concerned, life had presented a dead end. I'd had a brief taste of success and now . . . nothing. Back among the chickens and selling video equipment at weekend flea markets so I could pay the rent.

Depression set in. But hope returned when I learned that a group out of

the prodigal comes home

Lexington, Kentucky, called Couriers Unlimited needed a singer. I auditioned, got the job, and for the second time in less than a year, hauled my belongings to Kentucky—this time with my wife. But after only nine months, Couriers Unlimited broke up. I had less than twenty-four hours to grow depressed about a return trip to Wallace, though, because the next day, Ed Hill called to say that the Singing Americans wanted me back. So it was back to North Carolina, but at least not to the flea market.

Lisa and I continued to struggle. At the time, I didn't understand the enormous pressure that constant traveling puts on a relationship. It's like you can never get into a routine, never get quite comfortable with each other. Add to that our financial problems. Looking back, our complaints were typical of a lot of married couples. But at the time, I thought we had some of the same problems my parents had and that the way to deal with a dying marriage was to kill it with divorce. It was right around that time that my parents divorced, after Daddy found out Mama was having an affair. I'd seen lots of Christian artists divorce, too, and keep right on with their careers.

I had begun to think of my own marriage as a chain around my ankle, keeping me from happiness. And after less than two years, I was ready to get out the bolt cutters. That's exactly why, one day in the spring of 1984, I did one of the worst things I've ever done.

Lisa and I were at home in the kitchen, and I was leaning up against the counter.

"I have something to show you," she said. She put one arm behind her back and pulled out a gift box.

"What's this for?" I asked, trying to figure out if I'd missed a birthday or something.

"Open it," she said, smiling. She seemed excited, anticipating something, but I couldn't figure out what.

I lifted the lid off the box. Inside was a stack of tiny baby clothes.

"What is *this*?" I asked sarcastically.

"Look at it. What do you think it is?"

"You're pregnant?"

"Yes," she said.

I don't remember my exact words, but I said something horrible like,

"Great, with us getting along as well as we're getting along, now we're bringing a baby into it."

I remember the look on her face. She was broken, just crushed.

She should have slapped me right across the mouth. The only thing I can say in my own defense is that my nasty attitude didn't last for long. By the next day, I was falling all over myself apologizing to Lisa. That helped, but even my humblest *I'm sorrys* could never completely seal the wound. Still, after that I became the model husband—as much as a man can reverse a years-long trend over a period of months. When I look back now, I think that if I had treated my wife our whole marriage like I did when she was pregnant, as the Bible calls each of us to treat our wives, we would have had a great relationship.

I began pampering Lisa, shopping for baby clothes, planning the nursery, going to Lamaze classes, and if she wanted it, bringing her ice cream at two and three in the morning. We dreamed aloud together about what our baby would be like. I shared with her a recurring dream I'd been having since I was young: that I was walking along carrying a little girl on my shoulders. The little girl had blond hair and blue eyes, and we both smiled as I walked along. This dream always had a slow-motion, soft-focus quality and a sense of peace. But seven and a half months into the pregnancy, our peace was interrupted.

Lisa and I were getting ready for bed one night; she was in the bathroom and I was lying at the foot of our bed, my head propped on a pillow, watching TV. It was late, ten or eleven o'clock.

"Mike?" Lisa walked into the bedroom.

I tore my gaze from the TV. "What?"

"I think my water just broke."

"No way!" I said in disbelief. "We're still almost two months away."

"I know, but I'm pretty sure it broke."

I jumped up from the bed and started throwing clothes in a little duffle bag. The hospital was in Hickory, North Carolina, about twenty minutes away. I made it there in ten, keeping a lead foot on the gas the whole way. I helped Lisa into the emergency room, and hospital workers quickly checked her in and wheeled her back for an exam.

the prodigal comes home

A few minutes later, a white-coated, middle-aged doctor walked out to the waiting room. "Mr. English, I've examined your wife. It looks like you're going to have a baby tonight."

Tonight! My heart nearly stopped. Lisa still had almost seven weeks to go. In those days, premature babies didn't make it as often as they do now. "Is the baby going to be okay?" I asked the doctor. "Is the baby going to be okay?"

He wouldn't answer me yes or no, but instead gave me some sort of avoiding-malpractice-suit answer that meant exactly nothing. I didn't blame him for not committing, but it terrified me that he wouldn't give me any kind of prognosis. Suddenly I feared the worst—that the baby wouldn't make it, or she wouldn't be developed all the way, or she wouldn't be able to breathe on her own, or her brain wouldn't function properly. Or, or, or. Instantly, I blamed myself. The hall monitor God of my childhood was getting ready to punish me again. Hadn't I treated Lisa horribly when she told me she was pregnant? Hadn't I, even if for less than a day, not wanted this child?

I began to pray. I felt guilty about praying, because my prayer life had been awful. I'd fallen into the habit of treating God like some kind of errand boy, praying fervently only when I really needed to get out of a jam. That night I asked Him again to intervene. "I know this baby's coming early," I said. "And I know something wonderful could happen here, or something absolutely horrendous. Father, even though I'm not the best son in the world, can You please have mercy? Can You please let us have a healthy child?"

My faith was so weak that I wasn't even sure God could hear me. I was suddenly certain that it didn't matter that I'd dreamed of nothing else but the joy of having this little girl for more than two hundred days, or that I'd even dreamed of her while growing up. God was not fooled. He'd jotted down my earlier ugliness and was preparing to deal with me accordingly.

The doctor told me I could go back and see Lisa. I trudged toward the examination room carrying a truckload of guilt. Already nurses had hooked her and the baby to monitors, and I could hear the *whoosh-whoosh* of the child's heartbeat fill the room. I clung to that sound. As long as I could hear it, I knew she was still okay.

I told Lisa what the doctor wouldn't tell me—that everything was going to be okay. For the next two hours, nurses filed in and out, checking Lisa, announcing dilation measurements. I broke away to call my parents and hers, all of whom lived within a five-hour drive of Hickory. Within minutes, they'd piled into cars and were on the way.

Within two hours of our arrival at the hospital, nurses wheeled Lisa into a huge operating room. And the next thing I knew, the doctor said, "Push!"

I stood at the head of the gurney where Lisa lay, picturing a child born with no lips, no eyebrows, eight fingers, and twelve toes. I hoped for a normal baby but was afraid to hope. Then Lisa pushed one final time and I saw Megan: she seemed perfect, with a full head of fuzzy brown hair. The doctor suctioned her mouth, and she cried a tiny cry like the bleat of a lamb. Lisa and I burst into tears.

As nurses whisked Megan away to neonatal care, Lisa called out, "My baby! Is my baby going to be okay?"

Again the doctor wouldn't commit. "She *looks* okay," he said.

While nurses wrapped up things in the delivery room, I went to see Megan. I couldn't touch her in her new Plexiglas home. She lay curled in the incubator, the tiniest thing, only four pounds, ten ounces. Her skin was thin and wrinkly. Her arms and legs were spindly. She also had jaundice, so she looked yellow, like someone sick with a bad flu. She was the most beautiful creature I'd ever seen.

Two weeks later, we took her home. And for the first year, while we learned the ropes of parenting, Lisa and I invested ourselves in our daughter, too busy to think about ourselves. But after we got the hang of the mommy-daddy thing, it was as though we each said to ourselves, "Let's see . . . where were we? Oh yes, I remember: we were fighting."

+ chapter fourteen +

At home one day, the phone rang and Lisa picked it up. I had been walking into the kitchen when Lisa said, "A Gary McSpadden wants to speak with you."

I stopped dead in my tracks, then spun around as she held out the phone. "Do you know a Gary McSpadden?"

A Gary McSpadden? She might as well have asked me if I knew *a* Johnny Cash. Gary McSpadden was one of Southern gospel's great lead singers. He'd sung with the Statesmen and the Oak Ridge Boys, then, with another legend named Jake Hess, had formed the Grammy Award-winning Imperials. Now he was with the Gaither Vocal Band, and I'd seen them onstage at the Christian Artists' Seminar in the Rockies. They were the most perfect quartet I'd ever heard.

I took the phone, put my hand over the receiver, and whispered something like, "Omigosh-you-have-no-idea-who's-calling-me-here!"

A thousand thoughts sped through my mind. *Is he looking for somebody else I've been singing with — or is he looking for me?*

I swallowed and put the phone to my ear. "Hello?" And like it does when I get nervous, my voice shook. I *hate* that.

"Mike, this is Gary McSpadden."

"Hey, Gary, how are you?" I tried to act as cool as I could, but as Gary small-talked me for a few minutes, my mind raced.

the prodigal comes home

"I'm going to go ahead and get right down to the reason I'm calling," he finally said. "The Gaither Vocal Band has consisted of four people, with me singing lead, Bill Gaither singing baritone, Larnelle Harris singing tenor, and John Mohr singing bass. John has decided to leave."

Until he said that, I hadn't realized I'd been holding my breath. My chest deflated in a great silent whoosh. Gary was looking for a bass singer. I didn't sing bass. I looked at Lisa and shook my head in a way that said, "It's nothing, no big deal."

"So what we're planning on doing is not hiring another bass singer," Gary went on. "Instead, we're bringing in a new lead, I'll sing baritone, and Bill will sing what bass there is to sing. That brings us to you. We just wanted to see if you'd be interested in trying out for the part."

Does a chicken lay eggs? I told Gary that I was absolutely interested. He said the Gaithers would make arrangements for me to come to Nashville and audition. After we hung up, I grabbed Lisa and danced her around the room. I couldn't believe this was happening.

Bill Gaither had been a singer and songwriter since 1956 and, with his wife, Gloria, had built the Gaither Music Company into an industry. Starting out selling the sheet music to their own songs out of their home, the Gaithers tapped into a marketplace all its own. It wasn't gospel and it wasn't contemporary. It was "inspirational" music, and the Gaithers led the genre. Bill and Gloria, who'd both started out as English teachers, wrote huge songs, like "He Touched Me" and "Because He Lives," which now are sung all over the world. By the time Gary called me, the Gaithers had won enough Doves and Grammys to fill a good-sized trophy case. But Bill and Gloria were just these humble, earthy people—as real as you can get.

Within a few days after Gary called my house out of the blue, I found myself in the downstairs choir room of a big Nashville church singing for Bill Gaither. He sat down at the piano and played a few songs, putting me through my paces. When he played "Amazing Grace," I sang a verse, then Bill stepped up a key. I sang another verse, and he went another key higher. And he kept going up to see how high I could go. No problem. Back then, I could sing as low as a baritone if I had to and up high with the tenors.

Then Bill said, "Sing a little of that 'I Bowed on My Knees.' That's the song that made me want to call you." So I did.

While I was there, I also sang with Larnelle and Gary. Our voices blended well. Bill told me they liked me but that they wanted to hear me in concert. Suddenly the old fear gripped me. I flashed back to Tigers scout Art Meyers watching me wing a pitch into Mike Melville's head. If Bill came to a concert and I knew he was there, I'd choke. I just knew it. So I asked him for a favor.

"Would you do something for me?" I asked. "Let me give you a few concert dates and you come and see me at one of them, but don't tell me which one. I'll just do a lot better if I don't know you're there."

Bill understood perfectly and was very gracious. I left Nashville and went back to North Carolina. Then began a couple of the longest weeks of my life. I played four or five dates with the Singing Americans and heard nothing. Finally, one day, the phone rang. It was Gary McSpadden.

"The job's yours if you want it," he said.

At first I felt a rush of joy. But as it turned out, the decision was tougher than I thought. Things were going well for the Singing Americans. I'd had a number one song with "I Bowed on My Knees." I was up for Lead Vocalist of the Year at the *Singing News* Fan Awards, a competition I'd dreamed of since I was a boy singing with my family. Being nominated meant you'd made it in the world of Southern gospel. But the Gaithers weren't Southern gospel. They had an entirely different fan base. Was I ready to leave one style of music in which I had already climbed a good way up the ladder for another where I'd start again on the bottom rung?

Gary understood my dilemma. "Mike, it's up to you whether you want to be a big fish in a little pond or a little fish in a big pond."

I decided to call Bill Traylor who headed the record company where the Singing Americans had just recorded a new album, *Black and White*. I told him the Gaithers had offered me a job but that I wasn't sure I wanted to take it. He was very kind about it and said he'd call Charlie Burke and take his temperature.

It wasn't long before Bill called me back with good news: Charlie was ready to give me a raise to keep me. Lisa and I decided that if he gave me a decent one, I'd stay with the Singing Americans. Just to finalize things, we hopped in the car and drove over to see Charlie at his big office at the bus company.

He kept us waiting for thirty minutes. Finally, someone came out and told us he was ready to see us. "So I hear you got an offer to go with that Gaither group," Charlie said when we walked in. He didn't invite us to sit down.

"Yeah, Charlie. I guess you talked to Bill Traylor. Lisa and I have decided—"

"Well, I'll tell ya," he interrupted. "There's no more money to be given out. A raise is out of the question."

I was stunned. I had talked to Bill less than an hour before. What was going on?

"You ought to go on and join them Gaithers," Charlie barreled on sourly. "You'll probably fit in good with some of them folks anyway."

Lisa grabbed my hand and stared into my eyes, silently willing me not to react.

I swallowed a nasty comeback and said, "Well then, find yourself another lead singer, because I'm done." Then Lisa and I walked out the door.

+ chapter fifteen +

I remember riding out of Nashville one year after the Singing Samaritans put in an appearance at the quartet convention. I must have been about fourteen. All us boys were crowded into the van, and Daddy was steering east on the interstate, back to the North Carolina sticks. I turned around and looked out the rear window at the city skyline and imagined I could hear the heart of the music industry beating.

"Someday, I'm gonna come back here and make a living singing in this town," I said out loud.

As it turned out, I was right. In 1985 Lisa and I accepted the Gaithers' offer and packed our bags for Nashville. We could have moved to Alexandria, Indiana, where Bill and Gloria Gaither had been based for many years, but I chose Nashville, where Gary McSpadden lived. I wanted to be smack in the middle of the industry, especially since it would give me more opportunities to do studio work when I wasn't on the road.

It was Bill Gaither who renamed me. In promotions and album liner notes, I became "Michael" English instead of "Mike." Bill also quickly became my mentor, like a second father to me. I found out that we were both crazy about Southern gospel and that when Bill was a boy, he was as mesmerized as I was later by groups like the Statesmen and the Blackwood Brothers.

It still amazes me to watch Bill perform, to see him connect with an audience. He is just such a down-home guy, genuine, but brilliant too. He and Gloria met while they were both teaching high school English and quickly discovered that they both loved to write. Together they have written hundreds of songs, taking inspirational lyrics far beyond the traditional kind that looked mainly toward life in heaven. Songs like the award-winning "Because He Lives" connect with so many Christians because they talk about living victoriously in Christ right here on earth.

> *Because He lives, I can face tomorrow;*
> *Because He lives, all fear is gone;*
> *Because I know He holds the future,*
> *And life is worth the living just because He lives!*

As I began touring with the Gaithers, I soaked in their discussions of politics and theology. Gloria, still a teacher at heart, noticed the countrified way I talked onstage and tutored me on my grammar. At first, when she corrected me, I felt embarrassed about my backwoods upbringing and lack of education. But I soon realized she was just trying to help me improve my presence onstage.

In the early days, there wasn't a lot of work for me to do. At concerts, the Gaither Trio—Bill, Gloria, and Gary—performed for most of the show. Larnelle would do some solo material, and the Gaither Vocal Band, of which I was a part, would appear here and there. I would sing in maybe three songs per concert. At first this didn't bother me. Gaither events drew thousands of fans, and I was thrilled to play a part in such big events. I hadn't seen so many people crowd in to hear Christian music since the quartet conventions. But after a while, I became frustrated. With the Singing Americans, I had been used to singing pretty much through every concert, soloing on songs like "I Bowed on My Knees" and receiving standing ovations. I'm embarrassed to admit it now, but I didn't like being a little fish in a big pond. I wanted attention.

When the *Singing News* Fan Awards hit in 1985, I wasn't there. I was at the Gaithers' annual Praise Gathering in Indianapolis, a massive event that pulls in something like ten thousand people. While the rest of the Gaithers performed song after song, I twiddled my thumbs on the fringes, not doing much of anything. Meanwhile, Biney went to Nashville and accepted the honor of Favorite Lead Singer on my behalf. Disappointed and depressed, I flashed back to my last year in Little League when I was stuck singing in a little backwoods church instead of attending a baseball banquet and accepting a carload of trophies.

I grew increasingly dissatisfied, and Bill could see it. He called me in one day for a meeting. Lisa went with me. The handwriting was on the wall, we feared: Bill was going to fire me, and it would be back to North Carolina again, back to square one. When we sat down in Bill's office, he did in fact tell me that he could see I was unhappy. And he wasn't pleased that I didn't do much onstage, didn't connect with the audience. But Bill being Bill, he didn't fire me.

"Let me tell you what I can do for you, Michael," he said instead. "We'll find another member for the Vocal Band, but we'll keep paying you until something else comes along for you." That woke me up in a hurry. Here I was in the big time, and I was so wrapped up in myself that I was blowing it. I was pining away for accolades in Southern gospel instead of appreciating the opportunity God had given me and earning my way with hard work.

"Bill, if you don't mind, I'd like to try one more time," I said.

That turned out to be one of the best decisions I ever made. It changed my whole attitude. I said to myself, *I'm going to go out there, work hard, and appreciate my opportunities.* Where I had brought along my natural shyness to the Gaithers, I now began to smile more and open up onstage. Soon after that, I began soloing on a song called "Day Star," and audiences loved it. And gradually, through personnel changes in the group, I sang during Gaither events more and more. After two years with the group, things were finally looking up.

+ chapter sixteen +

When I first joined the Gaithers, I was making good money, but Lisa and I had moved from Small Town, America, to Nashville, Tennessee, so life became a lot more expensive. The Gaithers weren't traveling a lot at the time—Bill used to joke, "We're just a weekend group"—and I had a lot of time on my hands. After about a year, I started to go a little stir-crazy, so I decided I'd turn some of my extra time into extra money. Maybe start a college fund for Megan.

The music industry is like other creative fields. Sports photographers might do portrait work on the side to earn extra cash. Actors do commercials. Singers, even those with a regular gig, often do studio work. This can be in the form of demos (where you record newly written songs so that artists looking for songs can hear what they sound like) or background vocals for a group or singer doing a session.

In 1988 a singer named Mike Eldred invited me to sing background vocals on a solo project he was doing. I had met Mike earlier when the Gaithers were auditioning tenors. He didn't get the job, but he and I became friends and kept in touch. When his solo project came along, he needed two background vocalists, a man and a woman. He hired me along with an up-and-coming singer named Marabeth Jordan.

Marabeth's husband, Paul, also worked on the project as engineer, which is the technical guy who runs the sound boards and gets everything down on tape. A good engineer makes all the difference in the studio, and Paul had a solid reputation.

He also had a beautiful wife. Marabeth was a dark-eyed brunette who wore her hair in long waves that fell down around her shoulders. She had a big, brilliant smile so that when she walked up and hit you with it, you just felt . . . good. I didn't dwell on her looks, though: I was married to Lisa, she was married to Paul, and I liked Paul. Marabeth was just funny and sweet and easy to be around. She also had a rich alto-soprano voice and was serious about her craft. We became really good friends and that's all. At first.

By that time Lisa and I had been married for five years, and things had gotten pretty shaky. It seemed we fought about everything—and especially about money. I had started to wonder if maybe I hadn't gotten married too young. I'm not suggesting that getting married young is a mistake or that it justifies any unbiblical behavior. This was just how I felt at the time. The old problems had continued but seemed to deepen and harden around the edges as we fired at each other with the same old weapons.

Marabeth and I did a lot of work on the Mike Eldred record. Then other artists began hiring us as a backup duo. I'm not sure why—maybe they heard Mike's project and liked the way our voices worked together. That happens a lot in Nashville, artists hire the same sessions people again and again. Sometimes Paul would be part of the project, but often it would be just Marabeth and me, and we wouldn't know anyone else, so we'd go have lunch together. She used to laugh at me a lot—not *at* me, but with me, at the things I'd say. Guys like that. And pretty soon I started to find the attraction was changing.

I'd catch myself thinking about her a lot. Sometimes I'd stand in the studio watching her sing, thinking, *If she wasn't married and I wasn't married, what would it be like to be in a relationship with her?* Not just a sexual relationship. The whole thing.

This went on for several months. Then it began to consume me. Marabeth was on my mind constantly. I began to pray and ask God to take these feelings from me. They were wrong, I knew. I was coveting another man's wife, which is on the same list of sins as murder. But my prayers were like those of what James calls in the Bible "a double-minded man," a man who asks God for the wisdom to resist temptation but at the same time keeps flirting with the fire. I prayed that he would strip away my attraction to Marabeth. But instead of cutting ties with her, or maybe saying I was "busy" when a new studio job came up involving her, I stayed in touch. I even suggested her name to artists who needed a female vocalist when I was the one hired first.

Never was there a hint that Marabeth thought of me as anything other than a good friend. I thought it was all me. And there was no way I'd have told her how I felt, because I knew two things would happen: one, I'd lose my marriage, and two, I'd lose a good friend. Still, I felt torn apart inside.

One night after a session, I found myself sitting outside a studio in my car. Marabeth was still inside, finishing up a song. I thought about going back in to watch her sing. But I knew the right thing to do was go home. No matter how strongly I felt about Marabeth, I was already a husband and a father. Anything I did that led me anywhere other than home was wrong. Tears of frustration welled in my eyes. Then I started the car and pulled out of the parking lot. Driving through the street-lit neighborhoods, I fought the urge to burn a U-turn and go back. But once I got on the interstate, headed toward Lisa, I felt better.

Not too long after that, Marabeth joined the group First Call, and we lost touch. By God's grace, I had done the right thing. That time.

+ chapter seventeen +

Sometime in the late '80s, Gary McSpadden invited me to go to New York City with him to hear Brooklyn Tabernacle's famous two hundred fifty voice choir. Pastor Jim Cymbala is one of the most amazing men I've ever met, just so connected to God. He's a no-nonsense preacher, committed to compassion and unimpressed by celebrity. Single-handedly, he changed my view of what it means to be a Christian.

The sanctuary at Brooklyn Tab is huge, and Gary and I were seated in the front row. Before the service, Pastor Jim hurried down from the stage, squeezed in beside me, and pointed to a man sitting three or four rows behind us.

"See that man?" he said excitedly. "He had AIDS. He came in here dirty and broken right off the streets, but we loved on him, and now all his symptoms are gone."

Then Pastor Jim pointed to a skinny, dingy-looking man a few seats away from me. "That man came into the church last week high on crack cocaine. Ever since then he's been coming back, and we believe that God's going to deliver him any day now."

I couldn't decide whether to be appalled or amazed. I had grown up in a church where people expected you to clean up your act *before* you worshiped with them. It wasn't like they had specific rules ("Listen, y'all, if a crackhead comes in, usher him out"), but I believed to my soul that if a man walked into North East Pentecostal Free Will Baptist wearing a pair of shorts, the head deacon would've pulled him aside and advised him to go find himself some proper pants. So when Jim pointed out the crackhead sitting near me, part of me thought, *That guy's not even a Christian, and they're letting him sit on the front row? I don't want this dirty guy sitting by me!*

Brooklyn Tabernacle opened my eyes to a whole new world of Christianity: of loving your brother no matter what, feeding the hungry, clothing the poor. Pastor Jim didn't want a congregation filled with people who looked clean on the outside but were far from God in their hearts. It shocked me to realize that he would rather have the pews filled with repentant crack whores and street bums than with blow-dried hypocrites.

I was amazed by grace and appalled at my own thinking. Even after several years with the Gaithers, I still had not experienced a church like that, one that says, as dirty as you are, as deep as you are in sin, just come unto Me.

Brooklyn Tabernacle became one of my favorite places to sing, and it was there, around 1989, that I met Norman Miller, one of the great managers in Christian contemporary music. Neal Joseph, the head of Warner Alliance, a division of Warner Bros. Records specializing in Christian music, had come to Brooklyn Tab that morning to talk with Pastor Jim about the choir's next record. Norman had come along to keep him company.

If I had planned to try to impress a record executive, which I hadn't, I couldn't have set it up any better. First of all, I sang "I Bowed on My Knees." It's a slow, sort of traditional song that tells an incredible first-person story about a man who goes to heaven. He meets his loved ones who have passed on before him and sees all the patriarchs and famous saints. But that's not good enough for him. It is the second verse that really moves people:

> *I saw Abraham, Jacob, and Isaac . . .*
> *I talked with Mark, sat down with Timothy.*
> *But I said, "I want to see Jesus,*
> *Because He's the one who died for me."*

At Brooklyn Tab that day, that powerful choir came in with a huge gospel ending and just brought down the house. If songs were baseball players, "I

Bowed" not only would be the clean-up hitter but would hit a grand slam every time. It just never fails.

I didn't know it at the time, but Norman told me later that he had never been so moved by a song or an artist. Tears streamed down his face as I sang, he said. Afterward, he found me backstage and handed me his business card. "If you ever want to consider a solo career, give me a call."

Now, as you can imagine, solo and shy don't readily mix. I had always been part of a group, taking comfort in other performers, hiding behind a show. But after Norman approached me that day, a few other record companies did too. Lisa and I discussed it, and I got used to the idea of being on my own. Maybe it wouldn't be comfortable, but God often takes us out of our comfort zone into new adventures, new areas of ministry. A year passed as I thought and prayed about which offer to take.

When record companies first began approaching me to go solo, every producer said the same thing: "We know you can sing, but what do you have to *say*? What does Michael English have to *say*?"

That used to frustrate me to no end, because I didn't know.

"Get deep into the Word," I'd tell shiny new Christians. "Pray, study your Bible every day, and get connected with a good church." Not only was I not doing what I was telling other people to do, but I didn't have any idea what a good church was. I was in a different one every week. The thing about Christian ministry, especially the kind where you're onstage, is that you become sort of a professional Christian. Other people, even others in ministry, just kind of assume you've got your spiritual act together. They put you in charge of their congregations even though they don't know if you really even know Christ. The assumption is, if you're singing about Him, you must know Him.

Not that this was their fault. Remember, thanks to Daddy, I could *sell* it. I was even able to deceive myself. I thought, *Well, I'm singing, giving myself to the Lord's work. And there are people who tell me that my music blessed them or even caused them to give their lives to Jesus. I must be doing enough.*

But a secret voice deep in my heart told me I was a lot like the Christians in the church at Laodicea: lukewarm. "Because you are lukewarm—neither hot nor cold—I am about to spit you out of my mouth" (Revelation 3:16). It wasn't like I was living a terrible, sin-filled life. (I didn't even drink until I was in my thirties.) But I wasn't living a good, godly life either. Worst of all, I wasn't living *in relationship* with Christ. God was an *idea*, not my heavenly Father. Jesus was my Savior, but I didn't take up my cross daily and follow Him. Maybe that's why God decided I needed a bigger cross.

I don't know whether it was the pressure of the solo offers, my rocky relationship with Lisa, the constant, nagging inferiority I felt, or a combination of all three, but early in 1990, while driving down the road with Lisa, my world suddenly shut down. In an instant, darkness descended on me. I felt trapped in a tiny black room that shrunk to a closet, then shrunk further to a coffin. I swerved to the side of the road and stopped the car. Death surrounded me, crushing my chest. I couldn't breathe. I was sure I was having a heart attack.

"What is it? What's wrong?" Lisa asked me frantically.

I couldn't tell her. All I knew was that I was dying. When the feeling passed, I pulled back onto the road and kept driving. Lisa was mystified. I was terrified. It was *so real.*

The attacks kept coming, and they were unpredictable. They'd hit in movie theaters, on airplanes, at home, and worst of all, onstage. At Gaither concerts, I'd sit off to the side, waiting my turn to sing, and my heart sometimes felt like it would burst through my chest. I held my head in my hands, trying to ward off terror, straining not to lose it in front of an audience and flee from the stage. Bill knew I was struggling and was so compassionate, so sympathetic. My symptoms reached fever pitch on a Gaithers' tour through the western states. As our bus crawled up a steep mountain through a driving snowstorm outside Flagstaff, Arizona, fear of certain death gripped me again. *What if I had a heart attack right now? No ambulance could make it up here! We're completely cut off!*

That night Bill got me to a hospital. There, for the first time, I heard the term "anxiety attack." Later I was diagnosed with severe panic disorder, a condition that affects millions. Even with medication, for about six months the attacks completely took over my life. I didn't want to close my eyes because I was terrified that my heart would stop in my sleep. I didn't want to go outside for fear of freaking out in public.

Doctors helped some. But what really helped was a Christian friend. One night, Lisa and I went to Christ Church, and people laid hands on me and prayed for me. I myself got down on my knees and *begged* God to help me. One day a few weeks later, I was lying on the couch at home just after an attack when I heard a knock on the door. I heaved a huge sigh: a visitor was the last thing I wanted. But I dragged myself up and went to see who it was. Vicki Riley, a woman Lisa knew from church, stood on the porch looking at me through the storm door.

"Michael, can I talk to you for a minute?"

I smiled wearily and opened the door. "Sure, come on in."

I showed her back to the living room, and she took a seat on the couch. I sat across from her in an overstuffed chair.

"Lisa told me what you've been going through, Michael," she said. Then, as if she could read my mind, she began to tick off symptoms.

"Do you feel like you can *see* your heart beating in your chest?"

I nodded.

"Is it worse at night?"

Definitely.

"Do you feel like you're going insane?"

Absolutely.

She described to a tee my feelings of dread, of actively dying, of certain heart failure, of not being able to breathe. And as we talked, without my immediately realizing it, I began to feel better.

"Michael, I suffered for years from panic attacks," Vicki said. "But I have a grip on it now. I know how to talk myself down. So many people let it get ahold of them. You have to take control of it."

She was right. After I became a successful solo artist, magazines like *CCM* and *Guideposts* published stories about my struggle with panic disorder. I got many letters from people who had been struggling with this irrational terror but thought they were alone. I *still* get letters and e-mails. I used to stop and wonder, why did God give a messed-up guy like me a platform, a way to reach people? Then I realized it's the broken among us who can say to others who struggle, "Hey, I understand."

+ chapter eighteen +

Bill Gaither founded the Gaither Trio in 1956. By 1991, with twenty-two Dove Awards and three Grammys to their credit, Bill and Gloria were about ready to ride off into the musical sunset, take things a little easier, enjoy the grandkids. As one last send-off, Bill told Gloria that he'd like to get the Vocal Band together to "record one more southern gospel classic. I've always loved that style of music, so I'd like to have all my old heroes come in and sing on one song."[1]

Bill had no idea at the time that his idea would launch a mini-industry, the Gaither *Homecoming* series. He called in the Vocal Band, which by then was composed of Jim Murray, Mark Lowry, and me, for a recording session at Master's Touch Studio in Nashville. He also started calling all his old heroes: Jake Hess, founder of the Imperials; Hovie Lister, leader of the Statesmen; the Speers; the Rambos; the Goodmans—the list went on and on. All those old-time gospel stars gathered at the studio that day, and it was like a great big family reunion. Some of these people had met as teenagers, and now they were in their seventies and eighties. They'd had glory days and tough times, and some hadn't seen each other in decades. It was tough to break up the socializing to get them all into the studio to record.

Bill ushered the whole chattering group into the big room, and we all gathered loosely around the only instrument in the room, a grand piano. We were scheduled to record just one song, "Where Could I Go but to the

Lord?" But that one song spun a special spirit in the room. And when it was done, no one wanted to stop singing.

Again and again, one seasoned star and then another would call out another song to sing. And whoever was closest to the piano and knew the song would sit down and play it.[2] Tears flowed as these gospel greats relived the high points of their careers. I felt privileged just to be in the same room with all of these people who had literally written the soundtrack of my life. What I loved about it most was that these people were superstars in their time, as welcome among gospel music fans as movie stars are in Hollywood. But some had seen their best days and fallen on hard times. Some were struggling to muster up a concert where a hundred people came. Others were no longer singing at all. Most of the singers who were there that day have now passed on. It was God's perfect timing that Bill thought to gather them all together so that the world wouldn't forget them.

There was only one video camera in the room, brought along to shoot some tape just in case Bill wanted to use some clips on a Gaither Vocal Band video. I've seen accounts that make it seem like Bill was some kind of marketing genius—as though he had the deliberate thought, *I'll get a bunch of old Southern gospel stars together, shoot a video, and sell a million copies.*

Bill *is* a marketing genius, but the first *Homecoming* video was a fluke, a beautiful accident where all the on-camera chemistry just happened. When he played the tape back, Bill knew he'd captured something precious, a genuine piece of folk history. The *Homecoming* series went on to sell more than eight million copies, spin off television programs, and win Grammys. The Gaithers used some of the proceeds to establish the Gospel Music Trust Fund, a safety net for gospel singers and musicians who need financial help in hard times.[3] Best of all, many of the artists who had quietly faded away began to get invitations again to sing around the world.

You can't brag on Bill to his face; he'll just push it off. But Bill Gaither's crown in heaven will be extra heavy for what he did for those people. That's just the way Bill and Gloria Gaither are: they never give up on their friends. I couldn't have known then that I would soon need their friendship more than ever.

Michael English

JUST BEFORE THE *HOMECOMING* SESSION, I decided to sign with Norman Miller and Warner Alliance. Norman agreed to work on spec. "I know you're not making a lot of money right now, so I'll work for you without payment for a year," he said. "If by the end of twelve months, I can generate a hundred thousand dollars for you, you can pay me a percentage. If I don't, I won't take a dime."

It worked out in both our favors. My first album, *Michael English*, debuted in 1991 and eventually sold an astonishing two hundred fifty thousand copies. I don't remember exactly how much money I made, but I do know this: Norman and I both got paid. A lot.

Almost immediately, the fan mania began growing. Shortly after Warner released *Michael English*, I was doing a concert at a big church in Spartanburg, South Carolina. Before I went on, I was upstairs in the pastor's office where a huge window overlooked the parking lot. When I looked outside, I could see hundreds of cars locked in a traffic jam, all of them carrying people who had come to see *me*. Not the Singing Americans or the Goodmans or the Gaithers, just me. It was surreal.

It got even weirder after the concert. Some people from the church were guiding me toward a table that had been set up so that I could autograph CDs.

"Excuse me. Excuse me," I said, smiling as I tried to work my way through the dense crowd. I had almost reached the table when suddenly my head jerked backward and pain raked my scalp. I found out later that an overeager girl had yanked a bunch of hair out of my head. It was the kind of fan mania normally associated with boy bands. But I wasn't a boy. I was a married man, nearly thirty years old.

And I can remember exactly where I was when Norman called to tell me that a single off the record, "In Christ Alone," had hit number one: I was at the New Life Treatment Center in California, sent there by my record label after I leveled with Neal Joseph that my marriage wasn't working and I wanted out. The irony wasn't lost on me. I had a hit single declaring that Jesus was the sole source of my hope and strength, and here I was, halfway through a three-week course of therapy for depression.

I hadn't wanted to go. But Norman said I needed to try to work things out with Lisa. He was right, of course. But there was more at stake for all of us than the marriage. *Michael English*, my solo debut, was selling like crazy; a divorce would likely stop it—and my career—cold. I finished the therapy at New Life, in the process learning a lot about myself, such as that I was a follower and a pleaser, probably because I'd learned from Daddy that it was better to go along to get along. In therapy I learned to express my true feelings. And believe it or not, in a marriage, that's not always a good thing when those feelings are selfish and mean.

During therapy, I told Lisa I didn't love her anymore. After therapy, I told Norman I still wanted a divorce. Again, he encouraged me to stick it out. Not only was it the right thing to do biblically, he said, but my record label might drop me from Warner Alliance if I didn't.

+ chapter nineteen +

In February 1992, sitting at the Grammys among stars like Natalie Cole, Bonnie Raitt, and Sting, I felt I'd arrived. Warner Alliance had put heavy marketing muscle behind *Michael English*, sales were through the roof, and the album was nominated for Best Pop Gospel Album. Meanwhile, *Homecoming*, which I'd recorded with the Gaither Vocal Band, was nominated for Best Southern Gospel Album. *Homecoming* won, but my solo project lost to Steven Curtis Chapman's *For the Sake of the Call*. I was a little disappointed but not too much. It's true what they say about just being glad to be nominated. And two months earlier, I'd won three Doves—one for the Gaithers' project, plus New Artist of the Year and Male Vocalist of the Year.

I toured like crazy in 1992 and in December joined the cast of *Young Messiah*. Norman was the brainchild behind that project, the most successful Christian music production of all time. While Norman was growing up in Scotland, his family listened to Handel's original oratorio on their phonograph every Christmas season, working their way through a great big stack of 78 rpm records. As a boy, Norman loved it, and every year he looked forward to his parents taking him to Usher Hall in Edinburgh to hear it live. After he became involved in Christian music, he often wished he could find a version of *Messiah* that would appeal to modern audiences, "that my friends would enjoy listening to," he said.

In 1989 Neal Joseph put up the money to produce *Young Messiah*, and they took it on the road the following year with an ensemble cast of voices including Sandi Patti, Sheila Walsh, the Imperials, and Larnelle Harris. As the tour kicked off, Norman was terrified. He later told me he needed to sell nine thousand tickets per show to break even. It was an unheard-of number in Christian music. As it turned out, audiences averaged fifteen thousand per performance for *seven years*, amounting to more than a million people.

For a week in 1990, I joined the tour, filling in for Larnelle Harris, who'd had a death in the family. Then in December 1992, with my first solo record already a hit, I joined the regular cast. It was a plush tour, rock star stuff. We played arenas, traveled in a chain of luxury tour buses, stayed in nice hotels, and concentrated on performing. It was perfect touring, with an added bonus: you got to travel with your peers and get to know them a little.

One person I got to know was Twila Paris. She was very sweet and genuine, a real example of godliness, I felt. But I remember that there was a slight distance about her, as though she didn't want the people on the tour to get too close. These days I would say that's not a bad thing. On the road, thrown together in this kind of weird, surreal bubble and a long way from home, a certain wall needs to stay up.

Steven Curtis Chapman was on that tour with us, along with Sandi Patti, Wayne Watson, and Sheila Walsh, who is now a Women of Faith speaker— and Marabeth. First Call sang "Every Valley" on the *Young Messiah* record. Norman was their manager, and they were a regular part of the tour. At first it wasn't a problem. But after a while, the old attraction began stirring in me, and I began to notice Marabeth more and more—and notice her noticing me.

It's the road, the road. Touring can be a morally dangerous act. You're far from home. You're working, technically, but not really. As Dire Straits put it, "That ain't workin'; that's the way to do it." What you're really doing on a tour as well financed as *Young Messiah* is enjoying cushy travel from city to city, doing sound checks, singing, soaking up applause, signing autographs, and eating out. And if you're not grounded in your faith, you're liable to start believing you're entitled to all that Ritz-Carlton treatment. Throw in a troubled marriage, an old passion, and shallow faith, and you've got trouble.

Things were fine until Tulsa. But then there was this moment: Marabeth and I were standing around with a group of people in an office area at an auditorium at Oral Roberts University, where we were set to perform. We were all just shooting the breeze when I said something funny and Marabeth laughed. Then, at the end of the laugh, she said, "Oh Michael."

It was the way she said it, loaded with meaning, with intimacy.

A few minutes later, I pulled her aside. "That thing you did back there," I said. "What was that all about?"

She looked me in the eye. "Maybe one day, ten or fifteen years from now, I'll tell you about it."

Later that day, I asked her again.

"It's nothing," she said in that way women have that clearly means it's something. And I knew. I wasn't stupid. The next day, I called her room. "I need to know what you meant by that thing you did. It's driving me crazy."

We decided to go for a walk and agreed to meet in the lobby. From there, we headed out for a walking path that wound through the low hills behind the hotel.

"You're like a drug to me, Michael," Marabeth said as we walked side by side in the sun.

With my marriage in jeopardy, that was hard for me to hear, especially when I had been totally infatuated with her years before. During that walk, she told me that she'd felt the same way, even back then, but had decided to do the right thing. That stunned me, considering that I had struggled through the exact same conflict with the exact same result.

And she wanted to do the right thing now. "I love my husband, and I don't want to do anything to tear my family apart," she said.

"I know, Marabeth," I said. "I'm not asking for anything here. I just needed to find out what was going on."

We walked and talked and in the end decided that we weren't going to act on our feelings. Lisa, Paul, Megan, Marabeth's kids—too many hearts were hanging in the balance. Still, our walk lit a flame in my heart. As a man, I was thrilled to have a beautiful woman declare her feelings for me, to laugh at everything I said, to praise me, to *want* to be around me. It was intoxicating. I felt that chemistry, that excitement, the way you feel when you find yourself alone with someone you've dated for a little while and you know that any second now that first kiss is coming.

the prodigal comes home

Right there is where I should have gone to the Word, to the parts where it says to pray without ceasing, to put on the whole armor of God. I was vulnerable and in dangerous territory, and I knew it. And I was very good at pretending that everything was going to be okay.

"I've got this, God." I said to Him. "I can handle it. You can go deal with something else. I'm cool here." And the whole time I was saying it, I was thinking, *Will something happen? What if it does? What will it be like?* And I didn't mean sexually—although as a man, those thoughts certainly crossed my mind—I meant emotionally.

I also could have gone to my accountability group, a collection of people Lisa and I had assembled for just such occasions—pressures and temptations of fame and all that. But instead of looking at the group as something I needed, I looked at it as window dressing: something to do because that's what you did as a Christian solo artist. Looking back, I wonder how many of us fall into sin because we keep the truth from the people in our lives who could save us from ourselves.

And those feelings for Marabeth that electrified me—they were all a lie. Not that I didn't feel them. I did. I just didn't recognize those emotions as part of the deception that tears families apart. That Hollywood lie that tells us that "first kiss" feeling lasts forever with the right person. That I've-fallen-out-of-love-with-my-wife lie that is at the root of why people find themselves in marriage after marriage, searching vainly for that first kiss passion and throwing away real love with both hands. I didn't know then that real love is committing to your spouse for the rest of your life, enjoying the view from the mountaintops and hanging tough in the valleys, bonding together to become what God refers to in the book of Genesis as one flesh.

I didn't know any of that. So instead, I felt ripped off.

After our walk, and our decision not to act on our feelings, Marabeth and I acted on them. Not physically. We didn't touch each other. But we became extremely close, spending a lot of time together between performances. Other people on the tour started to notice, including Norman.

One day he pulled me aside. "Can I talk to you?"

"Sure, what's up?" I said.

"You and Marabeth are getting too close," he stated. "This is an unreal world on the road. This is not reality. You two need to be on different buses."

I was angry and offended, as a man often can be when he is not guilty technically but is guilty in his heart. In the end, we ignored Norman's good advice because we weren't "doing anything." But we were getting more and more emotionally involved. You could measure it by the minute.

+ chapter twenty +

The *Young Messiah* tour ended. Marabeth had remained faithful to Paul, and I had to Lisa. Technically, at least. But the close call scared me and seemed to help me get my priorities straight. I headed home with a renewed resolve to pour everything I could into my marriage. It wasn't the first time I'd made that vow in my heart to go full force with Lisa, to make our relationship work. Still, our relationship had disintegrated to the point where we had begun making decisions, such as whether to buy a bigger house, based on whether we thought we'd stay together.

Before the tour, Lisa had stood in the doorway of our little house in Antioch, Tennessee, and said, "Look, let's just buy a new house. If it doesn't work out, we'll sell it and split the money." So we'd taken the plunge and had a sprawling, 4,500-square-foot home built in Brentwood, a fancy suburb of Nashville. While we were waiting for it to be finished, we still lived in our little 1,245-square-foot tract home in Antioch. That's where I was on Sunday, January 3, 1993, doing what I do every time I get the chance: catching an NFL football game. I'm usually singing on Sundays, so it doesn't happen that often. But this was the first game of the playoffs, the Houston Oilers versus the Buffalo Bills, and I sat down with a bag of chips and a huge glass of sweet tea, ready to enjoy some smash-mouth football.

Unfortunately, the game was a total waste of time. Through the first half, the Oilers whipped the Bills like a whole family of red headed stepchildren.

the prodigal comes home

Quarterback Jim Kelly had gotten hurt the week before, and backup QB Frank Reich was stinking it up. At halftime, the score was Houston 28, Buffalo 3. Disgusted, I turned the game off. The next day I was sorry I had, because my friend John Stewart called to tell me that Frank Reich had engineered the greatest comeback in NFL history, beating the Oilers 41 to 38. But even more incredible was what John told me Reich had said at the post-game press conference: "Before I go any further, I want to read the lyrics to a song that really inspired me this week. The song is 'In Christ Alone,' and it's sung by the Christian singer Michael English."

Now, I am a sports *freak*. To hear that, honest to goodness, was as exciting to me as winning a Grammy. A few days later, Frank and I connected by phone, and he told me what happened that day and why "In Christ Alone" meant so much.

He'd felt the weight of the world all week. First, the Oilers match up was a playoff game: lose and you're out. Second, Frank had lost badly to Houston the week before, after Jim Kelly was injured and Frank had to take over the game. To add to the pressure, Kelly had taken Buffalo to the Super Bowl the two previous years. But with Frank starting in his place against Houston, the New York press had pretty much written off any chance of a three-peat.

The Wednesday before the Oilers game, his sister Cyndee called him and told him he *had* to listen to a song she'd heard.

"It's called 'In Christ Alone,' and it's by Michael English," Cyndee said.

As it turned out, Frank had an unopened copy of my first CD he had received from a radio station. "When I played the song, I can't even begin to describe how that song hit me in my heart very deeply," Frank told me. "There was so much pressure heading into that playoff game, and the words connected with me in a way that just overwhelmed me."

In Christ alone
I place my trust
And find my glory
In the power of the cross.
In every victory
Let it be said of me

My source of strength
My source of hope
Is Christ alone.

The morning of the game, he tore a sheet of paper from his playbook and wrote down the lyrics. "Then I prayed that before the day was over, I'd share those words with someone," Frank told me.

When game time came, he felt as energized as the crowd. But by the end of the first half, the stadium was like a tomb. The Oilers had shocked the home crowd into silence, piling up that 28–3 halftime lead. But in the second half, the Bills began to execute on offense. Frank connected on pass after pass, steadily closing the gap in the score. But he didn't let himself celebrate until Steve Christie nailed a 32-yard field goal to beat Houston in overtime in a game that still ranks as the biggest comeback in NFL history.

Before the post game press conference, Frank told the Bills public relations manager, "I'm going to read aloud the words to a Christian song that really inspired me this week. I know they're not going to like it. I know people will shut off their cameras and microphones, but I just have to do it."

The public relations manager laughed out loud. "Frank, we just had the greatest comeback in NFL history. You can say anything you want to say and nobody's going to turn anything off."

He was right. Frank walked in, raised a hand to hold back the usual flurry of questions, and said he had something to share. Then, with reporters scribbling and millions watching on TV, he read the lyrics he'd written down that morning and didn't stop until he read the entire song.

When Frank told me that story, I realized more than ever the incredible power and reach of music. I had no idea then that in a little more than a year, that power and reach would turn into a very public fall.

+ chapter twenty-one +

My second solo album, *Hope*, was released in 1993. While my management team worked to finish up the final details for the tour, Lisa and I put
all our time—and a ton of money—into our new house. At the time, it was
my dream house, and we hired interior designer Landy Gardner, decorator
of star homes and the Tennessee governor's mansion. Built of brick, its
double entry led into a towering foyer hung with an enormous wrought iron
chandelier. The huge island kitchen had white cabinetry with hunter green
walls and trim, two stoves with an open grill between them, and a breakfast
nook with white-shuttered bay windows. The pantry was ridiculous. We
laughed the first time we put food on the shelves; in the room-sized closet,
the few little cans looked lonely.

The first-floor master bedroom was the biggest room I'd ever seen, and
the master bath had a Roman soaking tub back before they were popular.
From the living room at the back of the house, a polished staircase wound
up to the second floor, where a railed landing overlooked both the living
room and foyer. Megan, eight years old at the time, said the staircase made
her feel like a princess living in a palace. And for me, it was a heck of a long
way from a house trailer in North East, North Carolina.

The coolest thing of all was the bonus room built above the three-car
garage. When we toured the model home and I walked into that room, I was
like, "Oh. My. Gosh. Just give me this room and I'll live here." They'd built
a sixty-two-inch television screen into the wall. That's a big screen *now*. Back

then, it was obscene. We had them build the bonus room in our house exactly like the model. I called it the Cat Daddy Room. Megan loved it.

Lisa and I still found time to fight, traveling some of the same territory we always had, like me always wanting to buy the best and her preferring less expensive choices. Still, we had a common project, a common goal, even if it was a material one. And we both enjoyed seeing Megan's delight as we brought home new treasures to decorate her palace.

When the sellout *Hope* tour began at Temple Baptist Church in Detroit, with the laser show and screaming fans, I felt I finally had life on track. My career was taking off like a missile. Things weren't perfect at home, but we were trying. The tour wound through city after city, and we played huge auditoriums. Everywhere we went, the fans were throwing babies out of the balconies. It seemed that even the Marabeth problem had resolved itself. First Call was on my tour as a separate group and also singing backup vocals for me. But from the beginning of the *Hope* tour, Marabeth and I stayed away from each other. There was a distance, a tension there. I wasn't sure what had caused it—maybe the fact that we hadn't kept in contact after the *Young Messiah* tour. In any case, I thought it was for the best. But in a bizarre reversal, the tension between us bothered others on the tour as much as our closeness had before.

One afternoon in the middle of the tour, I was sitting in an auditorium where the audience sits, listening to First Call doing sound checks. Norman came in and sat down next to me.

"Michael, would you go up and talk to Marabeth?" he asked. He just wanted us to mend fences, felt it might break the tension so the rest of the tour could wind up smoothly.

That night, when we rolled up to a Steak and Shake to get some dinner, Marabeth stayed on the bus. While everyone else went inside, I got some food to go and went back out to talk to her. We got things worked out, but it wasn't at all like we said, "Okay, let's rekindle something that's wrong." We just decided to try to deal maturely with the fact that we had felt a certain way about each other on the *Messiah* tour. And we agreed, for everyone else's sake, to try to get along for the rest of the *Hope* tour. What we should have done was stay as far away from each other as possible.

Instead, we started hanging out again, having fun, cutting up. Flirting. Nothing happened other than that, which was bad enough. Until the end of the tour. One Monday, we had a concert date in Raleigh, North Carolina. But we were off the day before, and that was the day I made one of the worst mistakes of my life.

"Let's spend the day together," I suggested to Marabeth.

She said she'd like that. So we rented a car and took off, went to a mall, ate, acted like teenagers. The next part is hard to talk about because it was downright rotten. I tangled with temptation and lost: I told Marabeth I wanted to get a room.

James 1:13–15 says this about temptation: "When tempted, no one should say, 'God is tempting me.' For God cannot be tempted by evil, nor does he tempt anyone; but each one is tempted when, by his own evil desire, he is dragged away and enticed. Then, after desire has conceived, it gives birth to sin." This was sin, pure and simple. It's so easy when you do something like that for the double-mindedness to take over. To say, *We'll get a room just so we can be alone, away from all those tour people. We can handle it. Nothing will happen.* But I knew inside I wanted it to happen. And once we made the turn to that hotel room, I crossed the line past the point of no return.

THAT WAS THE FIRST NIGHT Marabeth and I were together. The next night we were onstage together singing Christian music to a crowd of thousands. My hypocrisy burned me up inside; it was absolutely killing me to be up on that stage, basically lying to the people. At the same time, though, I wanted to see Marabeth again. I was, as the apostle Paul said, a wretched man trapped in a body of death, wanting to do right but also wanting to do wrong. And as is usually the case, doing wrong became easier as we went along.

For one thing, this wasn't like the *Messiah* tour. This was *my* tour. Norman flew in to catch a show or check on things sometimes, but there was no one else I had to answer to. Looking back on it, I can see I was on a bit of a power trip. *This* was the Michael English tour; I could do anything I wanted, and everyone else deferred to me because I was "The Star." There was no one who could hold me accountable.

the prodigal comes home

Poisonous stuff to a man with little spiritual grounding, a rocky marriage, and an ego that was growing by the second. Marabeth and I were together once more, maybe twice, on the *Hope* tour. But as the tour ended, we decided to end the affair. It was wrong, we knew. We decided to go home to our families. And we did. At first.

But after a week, I missed her terribly and called her. A couple of days later, we met in the parking lot of a Nashville restaurant. Sitting in my car, we were torn—attracted like magnets but knowing nothing good could come of what we were doing. We had to end it. Really end it. Have no contact.

But I was already entangled in sin, enticed by my own desire, and going down fast. The next weekend, I called Marabeth's cell phone again. First Call was doing a gig in Atlanta, and she was going to be there for a couple of days. The next morning, I had to be in the studio to record a song for a concept record. After that, Norman and I were supposed to meet for lunch. I didn't care. I told Marabeth I'd see her in Atlanta the next day.

On Monday morning, I called all the musicians and singers in early, met them at the studio, and rushed them through the session. I can't remember the reason I gave them, but I was impatient, throwing my weight around, acting like a diva, making other people bend to my wishes. When Norman arrived for our lunch appointment near noon, I was long gone. Two hours later, I was in Atlanta, in a hotel room with Marabeth.

When we'd talked on the phone about my coming to see her, we agreed it had to be the last time. And while I was there, we agreed again to go back to our homes, back to Paul, back to Lisa. I flew out that night and walked into my house with no good explanation of where I'd been. I can't remember what I told Lisa, only that whatever I told her was a lie.

But I hadn't been lying to Marabeth: I was going back to Lisa with a renewed determination to try again. Warner Alliance had already arranged for us to get off by ourselves for a week in Hawaii, all expenses paid. It was a chance for Lisa and me just to be together—no pressure, no concerts, no media, no phone calls.

Except for one.

Lisa and I were staying at the Sheraton Waikiki really having a good time—not hilarious, but more relaxed than we'd been in years. I had, as people do, buried my sin in my heart and worked hard at just enjoying our time together. Neither of us had ever been to Hawaii before, so we did touristy things—ate out in restaurants with lots of palm thatching, bought souvenirs for Megan, walked barefoot in the cool sand at the edge of the tide.

I think it happened on our fifth day there: I was up in the room clicking through voice mail messages on my cell phone, and I froze. I heard Marabeth's voice, sounding strained and urgent even on the recording: "Michael, you need to call me on my cell phone right away." I can't remember where Lisa was at the time, maybe out shopping on her own. But I know I went down to the lobby to find a secluded pay phone. I planned to call Marabeth back using a prepaid phone card. I didn't know what to expect. Had Paul found out? Had a picture of Marabeth and me turned up somewhere? In any case, I didn't want to leave a record of the call.

Looking back now, I hated the pressure of living a secret life. Of deceiving, of covering my tracks. The best part of true repentance, of holy living, is the ability to live a transparent life. But back then, I had to peer around the lobby, keeping an eye out for Lisa as I dialed Marabeth.

"I have something to tell you," she said when she picked up the phone. "And I don't know how else to tell you except that I've missed my period and I think I'm pregnant."

+ chapter twenty-two +

My heart dropped into my stomach in the exact same way as when someone sneaks up behind you and scares you to death. I couldn't believe what she was telling me. Here I was in Hawaii trying to patch up my marriage, and now here was news that could quite possibly change all of our lives forever.

"I'll be back in a few days," was all I could think to say. "Then we'll get together and find out for sure."

We hung up. Suddenly I felt my life was in free fall, completely out of my control. And all I could do was pray. It might sound crazy, praying to God to get me out of a mess like that. But don't we often do that? Ask God to take control only after we've held the reins of our lives in our greedy hands until it's too late? Why is it that we recognize only too late that God's rules—"Do not covet your neighbor's wife," for example—are given because He loves us and wants to protect us? If we prayed more for obedience, knowing the greatness of His love, we'd have to pray a whole lot less for deliverance.

But deliverance was exactly what I prayed for. I prayed the old, "Lord, if you'll get me out of this, I'll never, never, never do anything like this again" prayer. I also waited for my cell phone to ring, hoping Marabeth would call me back, tell me it was a false alarm, that everything was fine. I checked my voice mail again and again. But she left no messages.

Lisa and I had a couple of days left in Hawaii. The weight of one possible future sat on my shoulders like an anvil. I tried to act like things were fine between Lisa and me. But they weren't, of course. And now it wasn't because of *our* problems. It was because of *my* problem—one I alone had caused. On the long flight home, I knew the plane was heading through the skies at four hundred fifty miles per hour toward an entirely different life. If Marabeth wasn't pregnant, this scare, I felt, would be the thing that booted me back onto the straight and narrow. If she *was* pregnant, then life as my family— and others who depended on me—knew it, would end.

It was late April 1994. We got back to Nashville a few days before Gospel Music Association Week, with its rounds of press, events, meet-and-greets, photo shoots, and banquets. Lisa was in a great mood, encouraged by our time in Hawaii, which, of course, made me feel worse. In her blue eyes, I could see new hope for us, and I hated myself for it. I felt as though I were offering her a bouquet of red roses with one hand while I held a sledgehammer over her head with the other.

It took a couple of days before I could meet Marabeth. I don't remember what excuse I made, but I probably told Lisa I was going to play golf. That was a four-hour deal. Plenty of time to find out what I needed to know.

The day was so sunny it annoyed me. The delicate greens of spring dressed all the trees as I sped down the freeway toward Percy Warner Park in Bell Meade on the outskirts of Nashville. When I drove up to the park entrance, Marabeth was waiting for me in her car. We'd agreed she'd follow me into the park. I drove up the shaded, winding roads past picnic areas and fire pits, trying to get as far from any other people as possible. It wasn't like I was a familiar face to the whole town of Nashville, being known mainly in Christian music circles and among Christian music fans. But we were living smack in the middle of the Bible Belt with a church on every corner. I was terrified of running into someone whom one or both of us knew.

Finally, I pulled over in a secluded spot. Marabeth parked behind me and got into my car. I gave her a hug but not a kiss. "How are you doing?"

"Not too good," she said. Her worry cut vertical lines between her eyes, and she seemed close to tears.

"Did you bring a test?"

She nodded.

"Well," I said, "let's go find out how our lives are going to turn out."

I pulled up the road to a portable restroom. Marabeth got out of the car, went into the tiny brown hut, and came back out with the test in her hand, covered with toilet paper. She got back into the car.

"Give it here," I said. She did, and I held it, covered, in my hand. "Listen, however this turns out, we're going to deal with it. One way or another, we'll find a way."

Two minutes crawled by. We didn't talk much. Until we found out, there wasn't much left to say. I let another minute go by, just to be sure we'd waited long enough.

"I'm going to look first," I said.

I lifted the toilet paper and immediately laid it down again. And today, I can remember the exact words I said to Marabeth next: "Okay, now listen: it's going to be o—"

"Omigod! Omigod! Omigod!" she said, panicking and barely able to breathe. "I can't believe this! What am I going to do?" Marabeth threw her head back against the seat, then in one motion raised it up, reached for the door handle, and jumped out of the car. She stumbled away toward the woods, sobbing.

I got out of the car and walked after her. "Marabeth? We're going to find a way to deal with this. It's going to be okay."

She whirled around to face me. "Oh yeah, right! We're just going to go tell Paul and Lisa, and everything will be fine? It's *not* okay, Michael! It's not!"

I turned away, and for a few minutes, we drifted in separate directions, each lost in our own misery. That was the first time I really allowed myself to think about the consequences of what I had done. *What's Lisa going to do? What will Norman say? What about Megan? What about my little girl?*

+ chapter twenty-three +

The Dove Awards that year were held at the Grand Ole Opry, the home turf of legends like Larry Gatlin, Johnny Cash, and Patsy Cline. The famous venue that night was spangled with Christian music's best: Bill, Vestal, Mark, Twila, Larnelle. Steven Curtis Chapman was there, Michael W. Smith, and BeBe and CeCe Winans. These people didn't consider themselves stars, but they were stars to me—and friends. It made me sick to know that soon I would bring shame on them all.

Leading into GMA Week, people around me told me they thought I had a good chance to win in several categories, including Song of the Year and Male Vocalist of the Year, an honor I'd won the two previous years. But with the truth of my hypocrisy gnawing at me, waiting to be let loose like a pack of rabid dogs, the rumor I couldn't get out of my mind was the one about Artist of the Year. Norman thought I had a good shot at it. So did Neal.

And I desperately, *desperately* did not want to win.

For one thing, Steven Curtis had won Artist of the Year for, like, fifty-seven years in a row. Okay, I'm exaggerating, but you get the idea. Steven was *the* male face of CCM for a long time, and he is a good man. He has a beautiful family, is a great husband and father, and is one of the finest Christians I have ever known. I did not want to be in the same category as Steven Curtis—didn't deserve to be.

Second, Artist of the Year is the biggest award of the night. It's the last one presented, the one everyone in GMA waits for, the one newscasters focus on the next day. Artist of the Year means endless rounds of press interviews, and the last thing I wanted was attention. If I won, it also meant Norman's phone would be ringing off the hook with new opportunities. And since I knew that one way or another my career was basically over, there didn't seem to be much of point in that.

Even though GMA Week is a huge swirl of activity, the actual day of the awards is a day off. Lisa was so excited. She laid out her dress early in the day and planned to wear her long blond hair swept up and elegant with a pair of sparkling earrings she bought and loved. After all, it was her night too. We'd worked hard to get where we were, starting out in Podunk, USA, barely able to pay the rent and keep the lights on. While I traveled and toured, making jack-squat wages with groups like the Singing Americans, she was a faithful "keeper at home," as Paul says in 1 Timothy.

We may have fought about money, but at least I knew that every penny I made was accounted for, even when I wasn't making very many of them. When I was on the road, I knew Megan was safe and loved and well cared for. I knew other men whose wives paid more attention to shopping and socializing than to mothering when their husbands were gone, but Lisa was the best mom I'd ever seen. So as rumors swirled that I very well might sweep the Dove Awards that night, she deserved her fair share of the credit. I don't think she really thought about it that way. She just bubbled around the house like a teenager on prom night, sweet and unaware that her world was about to fall apart.

Meanwhile, on what should have been one of the most exciting days of my life, I felt as if I were wearing an overcoat made of dread. As we got ready to go, different people called me.

"Aren't you excited, Michael?"

"It's going to be a great night!"

I pretended to be happy. But inside I prayed silently, "Please, God, don't let me win." Isn't that crazy? Who would pray that? How could a man get himself into such a mess that the pinnacle of his career, the acknowledgment by his peers of his great "ministry" before God, felt like a walk into the valley of death? And as God would have it, that night was the Silver Anniversary telecast of the Dove Awards. Perfect.

Wrapped in an angelic white gown, Amy Grant emceed. Michael W. Smith kicked off the show with a bouncy pop song called "Love One Another."

Now, in the old days of awards shows, if you were performing or presenting, you pretty much knew you weren't winning. But by then the production formula had changed, and I rotated between the stage, audience seating, backstage, and the podium like a hamster on a wheel. I sang three different numbers, including one during which my life sort of flashed before my eyes. In a tribute to Southern gospel, I sang "I Bowed on My Knees." But I didn't sing it alone. Onstage with me, lined up left to right, were some of the idols of my childhood: Armond Morales, Vestal, and Jake Hess. Also with us was my mentor and dear, dear friend Bill Gaither, along with Larnelle and Mark Lowry, friends with whom I'd traveled many miles and learned so much.

Like a living memory album, my whole career was onstage that night. Including Marabeth. Whenever I was on, First Call sang backup. It was like that old television show *This is Your Life*, except this episode was from hell, with Satan as emcee, cackling, "This *was* your life."

The first award of the evening was Male Vocalist of the Year. I won.

"In Christ Alone" won for Song of the Year.

Recorded Song of the Year: "Holding Out Hope to You," from the *Hope* album.

Album of the Year: *Hope*.

Because a couple of the awards were presented before the telecast, I only had to make two acceptance speeches. When *Hope* won, I heaved myself out of my chair and walked up to the podium on legs that felt filled with sand. I looked out at the audience, at Lisa, beaming. I thought about Megan, with a sitter, watching at home.

"I want to thank some special people in my life," I said. "Thanks to Lisa for staying with me, even though I'm hard to stay with." *She has no idea* how *hard,* I thought. Then I looked into the camera and talked to my little girl. "Megan, honey, you can stay up all night long." The audience laughed, charmed by my good-dad act. I managed to squeak out a couple of other amusing comments, hoping to cover up my gloom. But people who watched the broadcast that night told me later that my head seemed to hang way down so that I looked as if I were carrying the world on my back.

the prodigal comes home

The night wound down quickly, uncontrollably, the way time always seems to pass when you're sliding toward known disaster. Because of the show's scripting, I happened to be standing backstage with BeBe and CeCe when it was time to announce Artist of the Year. My stomach was clenched in a tight, hard knot. Then Amy introduced the Winans. And as soon as they stepped out onto the stage, I started jabbering.

I don't remember who I talked to or what I said. I just talked and talked and talked, hoping to block out what was happening onstage. I was completely conscious of what I was doing: pretending just for that moment that none of this was happening. That if I just kept talking long enough, the rumors wouldn't be true, I wouldn't win, it would all go away.

Then I felt someone tug on my arm. "Michael! You won! You won!"

Now it's going to get really bad, I thought. Then I twisted my lips into a weak smile and walked out under the burning lights.

+ chapter twenty-four +

The Grand Ole Opry thundered with applause, and my heart thundered with it as BeBe and CeCe waited for me to reach them at the podium. BeBe gave me a great big hug. *If you only knew,* I thought as we embraced. Then I turned to the podium, my head low, wavering on what to say. I had given a lot of thought to this moment. Leading up to awards night, I had played with the idea of giving a retirement speech instead of an acceptance speech. Something like, "I want to thank everybody for everything they've ever done for me. But I've gone my last mile. I'm ready to say good-bye and start a new chapter in my life." I contemplated doing that even up to the moment I won, but in the end I couldn't do it. If I had said that, I would have stunned too many people all at once and would have had to start answering questions I wasn't sure I wanted to answer yet.

I put both hands on the podium, and because of my height, I had to bend to the mike. "This is, uh, this is the most incredible thing that's ever happened."

My voice felt at the edge of tremors, but I was able to hold it together. "I mean, I can't imagine this happening tonight. . . . I've got just a few people I need to thank tonight, especially Bill and Gloria Gaither. I know I wouldn't be on this stage tonight if it wasn't for them tutoring me, teaching me, showing me the way."

My heart felt like it was going to pound out of my chest. As I had the other time I came to the podium, I had to say something light, *had* to, the way trauma workers crack jokes to keep from cracking into pieces. Everybody knew by then that I always sang with gum in my mouth. "I'd like to thank my gum," I said, "for providing me with enough saliva."

Big laugh from the crowd. Inside, I cringed. "I just can't believe this is happening," I fumbled on. "It's been a wonderful few years, and God has blessed—"

My throat tightened as though gripped by a giant hand. I couldn't speak. I looked out at the audience, so many of them my friends, my heroes, my mentors. In that moment, I knew it would be the last time I'd ever see those people from a Dove stage. Everything I'd worked for, every struggle, every time I'd overcome the thought that I wasn't good enough, every time I'd wrestled down my certainty that I really belonged up in the balcony watching everybody else down here—I had crushed all that in what really amounted to a few days. You couldn't even count my affair with Marabeth in weeks. I thought, *You, Michael English, are a stupid, stupid man.*

All this flashed through my mind in an instant. I dropped my head. Dead air filled the Grand Ole Opry and the telecast. The silence lasted only seconds, but it seemed like forever. I willed my voice to work and raised my head just high enough to be able to speak into the mike. I could barely squeeze out my last words. ". . . and I hope I'll continue to do what God wants me to do—whatever it is. Thank you very much."

The audience burst into applause. Then, like a walking dead man, I headed back to the stage for the final song, "We Believe in God." *Everyone* was up there. It was like the Dove Awards version of "We Are the World." I stood next to Bebe. Michael W. Smith, Twila, and Amy sang nearby. My stomach turned as I voiced the lyrics. And I knew it wouldn't be long before some of the people up there, so happy to share the stage with me that night, would very shortly wish I would disappear.

+ chapter twenty-five +

If there hadn't been a baby, Marabeth and I might have made our mistakes and suffered, as Paul says in 1 Corinthians, the internal consequences of sinning against our own bodies. As much as I hate hypocrisy, I might even eventually have confessed to Lisa. None of that would have made my wrongs right, but all sinners can do is turn from their sins. Only God can erase them.

But now there was a baby, a new life that added urgency to the situation. Never did Marabeth and I discuss running off and leaving Paul and Lisa. But something had to be done. And whatever we chose, I realized that life as I knew it would come to an end. On the one hand, I thought that maybe, just maybe, we might be able to do something to clean up this mess. Bill Gaither had once made a statement to me about sin: When a brother goes through something, the shame of what he has done is enough. We don't need to keep shaming him. In other words, some music minister in Small Town, USA, did not need to hear about Michael English's moral failure. Instead, it should be handled privately to protect the ministry.

On the other hand, I couldn't stand the accolades. I couldn't stand the thought of being praised as Christian music's top artist. I didn't deserve it and burned with shame that artists who had ministered faithfully were passed over in favor of someone who had betrayed them all.

Whatever happened, I had to tell Lisa. The day after the Dove Awards, I

the prodigal comes home

telephoned a friend of hers—I'll call her Michelle. I wanted Lisa to have someone there to support her.

"Michelle, I need you to go to the house," I said when she picked up the phone. "Don't ask any questions. I just need you to be there for Lisa. Can you go?"

"Yes . . . ," she said, sounding puzzled.

"It's very important that you go there right now. Please don't ask any questions. You're going to find out soon enough."

I went and picked up a friend of my own, Brian Hudson, and we drove to my house. Lisa was there alone; Megan had gone to visit a friend. I told Lisa I needed to tell her something, and she, Michelle, Brian, and I gathered upstairs in the Cat Daddy Room. Her face strained with concern, Lisa took a seat on the couch against one wall with Michelle standing near. I knelt at Lisa's feet, and Brian stood behind me. The huge house spread around us, as still and silent as a morgue.

This is how quickly it happened: "What is it? What's wrong?" Lisa asked. "Has something happened to Mom?"

"Your family's fine," I said. "Lisa, I don't know how else to say this, except that I've had an affair, and the result of that is there's a baby."

Michelle's mouth fell open. Lisa sprang up from the couch, screaming, "Who is it? Who is it?"

Brian clapped both hands over his mouth and nose, his eyes wide. Lisa began shouting names, trying to guess the identity of the woman. I tried desperately to get her to sit down.

"Who is it?" she yelled again, reeling off more names. "Who is it?"

"It's Marabeth, with First Call," I said.

"I can't believe this!" Lisa screamed, rightfully outraged.

"Lisa, I don't know what to say. I don't know what to do!" I pleaded. "I'm sorry. I'm so sorry."

Yelling and now crying, Lisa forced her way off the couch. Then, as God is my witness, Michelle started praying in tongues.

I pinned her with a glare. *"That's. Not. Helping!"* I said, biting off the words.

But it didn't matter: Lisa stormed out of the room.

BRIAN AND I LEFT THE HOUSE, met up with Marabeth, and went to tell Norman. After all he'd done for me, after all his hard work to turn me into a solo success, can you imagine him being hit with this kind of news?

But sitting in his tasteful living room, he gave me the typical low-key Norman speech. "Michael, Michael . . . oh Michael, what have you done?"

He tried to come up with a plan of action. I could take a year off, he suggested, get some therapy. Looking back now, I think, *Why didn't I do that?* As terrible as it is, here's the answer: because I wanted out. I was ready to end my marriage, and if my career had to go too, I thought, so be it. I had *already gotten therapy.* I felt at the time that I had tried and tried and tried with Lisa. To the world, it looked as if everything in my life was going great. But I knew that my personal life was terrible. I was sick to death of the fighting and the faking.

I look back now and think, *So what?* In marriage you persevere. It's that simple. But I'm a better man now than I was then. Then, it seems I was bound and determined to fulfill the childhood prophecy that I would never amount to anything. I was *ready* for self-destruction.

For several days after I broke the news to Lisa, the atmosphere in our home was like the week after a funeral. Our friends John and Suzanne Stewart spent a lot of time there, consoling us, praying for us. People came, brought meals, and quietly left. Our pastor, L. H. Hardwick of Christ Church, came to offer prayer and counsel. I appreciated Brother Hardwick's coming, but I felt so guilty and ashamed that I heard him without really listening.

Norman, meanwhile, called a meeting at his home. His purpose was to save both our marriage and my career, but to me the meeting felt like an ambush, and I went in loaded for bear. Two things were driving me. First, as I said, I still wanted to end my marriage and I'd found a way out. The second thing, related to the first, was this: I had been managed since I was ten years old. All my life people had been telling me what to do, where to go, how to sound, how to act. From little things, such as the length of my hair, when to raise my hand while singing, and whether I could go accept my own baseball trophies, to big ones, such as my next career move and whether I should stay in what I thought was a failing marriage. My recent success in music had led me right to the edge of having at least a little control. Now the authority and the moral standing to call my own shots had evaporated—instantly. But I was too angry and proud to acknowledge, that, and, like a fool, I picked that meeting to make my stand.

Six of us were gathered in Norman's living room: Lisa and I, Paul and Marabeth, Norman, and Scotty Smith, pastor of Christ Community Church, Nashville's unofficial pastor to Christian artists. The tension humming through the room was so intense that I felt if I had some sort of special glasses, I might be able to see sparks shooting through the air between the traitors and the betrayed.

Scotty opened the meeting with a prayer. I can't remember who spoke next, but soon Paul spoke up. "Maybe it would be easier," he said, "if Marabeth is prepared to stay with me, I adopt the baby and we raise it as our own."

It was an astonishing, incredibly gracious thing to say. But in that meeting I was an astonishingly incredible jerk.

"This is *my* baby!" I yelled. "Marabeth, you can stay with me if you want to—that's fine! But nobody else is raising this baby!"

Lisa sat beside me, tears welling, devastated. In one sentence, I had stripped her of her rightful place, filled it with another woman, and declared that I would begin an entirely new family without her. My words must have pierced her heart like a dagger.

Scotty counseled me not to be too quick to reject Paul's suggestion. Norman quietly repeated the plan he'd laid out earlier: I should take a year off, reconcile with Lisa, and get some counseling. In his way, he was trying to save me. But I didn't want to hear it. My attitude was, *You're not going to tell me what to do! You're not!*

Surrounded by clouds of confusion too thick to see through, at a time when I lacked wisdom and really needed someone to *please* tell me what to do, I lashed out instead. I was mad at the world, pointing the finger at everyone in sight. I have often thought if I could go back and confront myself on that day, I would slap the crap out of me.

+ chapter twenty-six +

The meeting established nothing (except that I was out of control), and the next several days passed in a blur. We hadn't yet gone public with the affair. But Norman told Neal Joseph about it, and Neal called me in for a meeting, at which he told me he was going to freeze my contract. Neal also wanted me to release a public statement. We drafted and released it on May 5, 1994:

> I feel it is necessary to announce my withdrawal from Christian music because of mistakes that I have recently made. Although I am very appreciative of the support I have received from those involved in Christian music, I feel it is necessary to relinquish the Dove Awards that I was honored with this past week.
>
> To Warner Alliance and the GMA, I am sorry. I am a human being. These circumstances are obviously the hardest I have had to face in my life. And I would hope that you will support me and all of the persons involved with your prayers.

Ashamed and feeling I'd betrayed my fellow Christian artists, I asked John to return the Dove Awards to GMA. He wrapped up all six of them in newspaper, put them in a cardboard box, and drove them over to the group's headquarters. But GMA president Bruce Koblish sent them back, then called me. "You earned those awards, Michael," he said. "There's no moral clause that says you have to turn them in." He also told me he was praying for me.

the prodigal comes home

After that, the media swarmed like piranhas at a buffet lunch. What could be tastier than Christian singers caught in an adulterous sex scandal? Never mind that our lives were collapsing around us; news vans camped on our street, print reporters roamed the neighborhood on foot interviewing anything that moved, and broadcasters delivered stand-up reports with our house as their backdrop. At one point, the crush of media triggered a panic attack. I couldn't find Megan and freaked out.

"Megan! Megan!" My voice echoed through the huge house as I ran frantically from room to room. Where was she? I couldn't find her! Had she been playing outside and been trapped by a reporter looking for a tear-jerking scoop? Finally, Lisa, John, and Suzanne calmed me down. Megan was safe, spending the night at a friend's house.

She was only nine years old. We put off telling her anything for as long as we could, wanting to shield her and, at the same time, not knowing how in the world to drop such a life-shattering bomb on a little girl who treasured her mama and daddy both. Finally, as news coverage boiled over like a pot with the lid on too tight, we decided it couldn't wait any longer. We took her to John and Suzanne's house, which was comfortable and familiar territory because we had spent a lot of time there over the years.

There we arranged ourselves in the den in front of the fireplace, left cold since it was May. Lisa and I sat on a couch with Megan between us. Suzanne sat in a chair to our left, and John remained standing. It was one of those times in life when you don't know how to say what needs to be said. So you just pray, open your mouth, and hope the right words will come.

"Megan, honey," I began, "we have something to tell you. We want you to know that no matter what, we love you."

I paused, not sure how to explain to my precious little girl that I'd betrayed her and her mother with another woman. In the end, I decided to keep it at a level I thought she could understand.

"Daddy's made a big mistake," I went on. "It's going to be out, and people may try to say something to you about it at church or different places. No matter what you hear, I want you to know that *it's not your fault.*"

No, it's your fault, my mind screamed at me. *And you can't undo it. You can't undo what you've done to this innocent little girl.*

Tears appeared at the corners of my eyes, and Lisa began to weep. "All you need to know is that we're always going to love you and we're always going to be here for you," I said, and my voice broke. "Daddy's sorry, Megan. Daddy's so sorry."

Then Megan English did something that still breaks my heart when I think about it. She stood up and walked around behind the couch, reached over, and wrapped her arms around my neck.

"Daddy, it's going to be okay," she said, holding me in a tight hug.

Everyone was crying then. "It's not supposed to be this way," I whispered. "I'm supposed to be consoling her, not her consoling me." Still, I held on to Megan's little arms and wept.

+ chapter twenty-seven +

It didn't take long before a couple of kids at school began to taunt her.

"My daddy saw your daddy on TV," one child told Megan.

"I don't care!" she snapped back. "You don't know *anything* about my daddy!"

When we had to pull her out of school for a while, the far-reaching reality of my sin began to trickle down to innocent people. Norman, for example. When I refused to repent, he quit as my manager. Then, trying to save face, I fired him.

Over and over, I saw myself on television. The channels rebroadcast my last speech at the Dove Awards as though it was on an endless loop. The national media picked up the story, and soon, instead of the music pages, I'd made the news pages in *Newsweek*, the Associated Press, the *Singing News*, and worst of all, the tabloids, where one story about a high-profile Christian hypocrite was worth ten about aliens invading Detroit.

During this time, I did a lot of driving around, just thinking, trying to sort through the mess I'd made. One evening I pulled over in a little park in Brentwood, not far from my house. I just wasn't ready to go home. I hadn't been sitting there long when my phone rang. It was Mark Lowry.

"How you doing, Michael?" he asked.

"I'm hanging in there," I said. "I don't know where I'm going to go or what I'm going to do, but I'm . . . hanging in there."

"Somebody wants to talk to you, and I wanted to make sure it's okay," he said.

Puzzled, I said it would be fine and hung up. The phone rang again, and it was Michael W. Smith.

"Michael, I can't begin to know what you're going through," he began. "I'm not here to judge you or anything. I just want you to know I'll be standing in the gap for you."

We talked for a few more minutes, and he was so gracious. It wasn't like he was taking sides or condoning what I'd done. He just wanted me to know he was praying for me. I've always appreciated that.

Other people also reached out to me. Naomi Judd, the country singer, and her husband, Larry Strickland, called me one day. They had a condo in Brentwood, they said, and offered to let me stay there. I knew Naomi and Larry, and also Naomi's daughter Wynonna, from Christ Church. It meant a lot to me that they stood in there with me when it seemed that so many others mainly pointed and whispered. Larry also offered to manage me. We had a lot in common. He's from North Carolina, not too far from where I grew up. While I was singing with my family group, he was with a quartet called Glory Road and later went on to sing with J. D. Sumner and the Stamps.

I moved some stuff over to the condo. Marabeth was still carrying the baby, but we hadn't made any decisions about our relationship yet. I was driving through Nashville in my Bonneville one day when the phone rang.

"Michael, it's Mike Curb." Mike is president of Curb Records, a successful country label that was then home to artists like Wynonna, Hank Williams Jr., and Sawyer Brown.

We exchanged the usual warm-up greetings. Then Mike said, "I hear you think your life is pretty much over."

"Pretty much," I agreed dully.

"Well, I'm here to tell you that it's just beginning. I'm here with Larry Strickland, and we're talking about what to do with you. I'd like you to come in, and let's talk."

Ironically, having someone discuss "what to do with me" didn't seem as irritating as it had when I grandstanded at Norman's house. In fact, I saw it as the first ray of hope, for my career at least, since all this had happened.

In the music industry version of a fire sale, Mike bought the rights to all my songs from Warner Alliance. Ironically, my record sales shot up for a time after the news broke that I'd turned in the Doves. I was surprised when Christian radio stations that banned my songs got a slew of angry phone calls.

But for every door that opened, it seemed another one shut. I called a Christian PR agency and asked if they would handle me. They turned me down. A major record distributor owed me $50,000 but refused to pay. They had a morality clause, they said, and were expecting a lot of Christian stores to return my records. The *Singing News*, a periodical that covers Southern gospel, began censoring my name. I found out about this when a young artist told me that in a *News* interview, he'd named me as one of his major musical influences.

"They took that out," the singer told me.

I thought, *Man, it's one thing to suffer the consequences of sin. It's another to be written out of history.* I had made some significant contributions to Christian music, for one thing, helping to bring Southern gospel to a whole new audience. *Punish me,* I thought. *But don't erase me.*

MARABETH WENT HOME to her parents' house in Arkansas to sort things out. It was from there that she called me to tell me she'd miscarried. Was it the stress of scandal? I don't know. Some people had praised Marabeth and I for coming clean instead of quietly aborting the baby and going on with our lives. That had never even been a consideration. It was ironic that now there was no baby, but all our lives were ruined just the same—and for what turned out to be just a few brief hours of very costly pleasure.

After weeks of indecision, I told Lisa I wanted a divorce.

"I just don't think I want to do this anymore," I said, standing on the back deck of the Brentwood house, delivering the news to her door like some kind of heartless mailman.

Lisa stood framed in the doorway. "If that's your decision, there's nothing I can do about it," she said softly, her eyes filling up with tears. "I'm sorry you've decided that."

the prodigal comes home

After that, Marabeth and I decided to make a go of it. It lasted less than six months.

MEANWHILE, IN HIS TYPICAL STYLE, Bill Gaither stuck by me. He wasn't flashy about it. He was just his steady, compassionate, fatherly self. "We're going to get through this, Michael," he told me, referring to the scandal I'd created.

As a vote of confidence, a way to show me that he wasn't a man who would turn me out, he hired me to produce the Gaither Vocal Band's new album, *Testify*. A singer named Buddy Mullins had replaced me as lead in 1993, after my solo career took off. *Testify* would be the Gaither Vocal Band's first album since. The job of producing it was bittersweet, since the reason I'd left—a soaring career as a solo Christian artist—no longer existed.

If it hadn't been for that record—and a toy poodle named Pumpkin—I might never have met Missy Council. I had just bought the puppy as a present for Megan. She and I had wanted a dog for a long time, but Lisa didn't want one in the house. I had taken Pumpkin to the studio that day because he wasn't potty-trained and was too young to be left alone in the condo. Besides, no matter what I did, I couldn't get the little thing to eat and I was starting to get worried.

On a break, I took Pumpkin out to a lounge area, set down a bowl of puppy food, and practically set the dog in the dish. "Eat, puppy . . . eat!"

But just as he had at home, he sniffed at the food, nibbled at it, then spit it out. I couldn't figure it out. What was I doing wrong?

Just then, a young blond woman came into the lounge. Never having owned a puppy and desperate for help, I turned and looked at her. "Excuse me, can I ask you a question?"

"Sure," she said.

"Why isn't this dog eating?"

The woman walked a little closer and took one look inside Pumpkin's bowl. "You have to soften a puppy's food," she said matter-of-factly. "Put a little warm water in it. That ought to help."

I felt silly for not having thought of that myself.

We introduced ourselves, and I learned that she was Missy Council, an old friend of Buddy's. It turned out that Buddy's dad was a pastor who had preached revivals all over the country, including Paducah, Kentucky, where he became good friends with a pastor named Topper Council. As a result, Buddy had over the years become good friends with Topper's daughter, Missy. By 1994 Missy had graduated from Murray State University and moved to Nashville to pursue a paralegal career. Buddy knew that Missy was a big fan of my music, so when he heard I was producing the new Gaither record, he invited her to come down and watch me work. And here we were.

"Hey, would you like to go out with my friends and me sometime?" I asked her, not looking for a date. I just liked her straightforward attitude. She seemed real.

"I'd love to," she said.

Then she added, "Michael, I know what you've been through, and I don't judge you. I just want to be your friend."

Missy Council quickly became one of my best friends. Years later she would save my life.

+ chapter twenty-eight +

A couple of months passed. The most painful thing was missing Megan, going days without seeing her, not putting her to bed at night, not wrestling with her after school—holding her down and tickling her face with my beard until she sputtered with giggles. I slipped into depression.

Then while still staying at Larry and Naomi's condo, I came down with an absolutely deathly flu. It wasn't a cold or a respiratory infection or bronchitis. This flu was one of those that drills down into muscles and bones until just to be awake is to be in pain. Tylenol didn't help. Motrin didn't help. Desperate, I dragged myself to the bathroom and rummaged around in my medicine cabinet until I found a bottle of Loritabs, a serious painkiller. I had a few tablets left over from a medical procedure I'd had some years back. I took one and within forty minutes felt I'd returned to the land of the living. My brain also registered and filed away an interesting side effect: I didn't feel depressed anymore.

One day not long after the flu passed, I was driving to a session in downtown Nashville when my cell phone rang. "How would you like to do a duet with Wynonna?" Larry asked me. "The song would be the lead track to a movie with Richard Dreyfuss."

My answer was, basically, "Where do I sign?" I was ready for some good news.

It was funny: after I found out Marabeth was pregnant, I had confided in Wynonna Judd over dinner at a Nashville restaurant called Houston's.

the prodigal comes home

Wynonna is a Christian. At the time, she was also unmarried and pregnant, a fact that would eventually make the papers. Meanwhile, I was a Christian who had gotten someone else's wife pregnant. We shared our troubles over sweet tea and green salad with hot bacon dressing. Later, after the world learned about both of our sins, a small Nashville paper published a remark that went something like this: It's so "Nashville" when "Michael English has a baby out of wedlock and it destroys his career but Wynonna has a baby out of wedlock and it helps her career."

The point, of course, was that I was a "Christian singer," while Wynonna was a singer who was a Christian. Plus, she was a country singer—in country music, when your dog dies, your truck breaks down, or you become a single mother, you back up, regroup, and write a hit song.

As it turned out, the Richard Dreyfuss movie was *Silent Fall*, and the duet with Wynonna was called "Healing." I got the gig and was happy about it. Guy Roche, an up-and-coming producer-songwriter who would go on to work on films like *What Women Want* and *A Walk to Remember*, flew out from LA to produce the song. "Healing" didn't do a whole lot on the charts, but it was my first experience doing secular music. I enjoyed the high production value and was grateful for the chance to sing. The project gave me a mental boost: *It's okay*, I thought. *I'm knocked down, but I'm not out.*

Not long afterward, Mike Curb chose a group of my songs that were less "Christian" and more pop-oriented, including my duet with Wynonna, and put them together on one CD. The label released it in 1995 under the title "Healing." The title was appropriate. That really got me out there. It got me started again.

AS THE POSSIBILITY OF A NEW and different career took shape, a new and different social life shaped up as well. I started going out to the best nightclubs in Nashville and received an enthusiastic welcome. People not only didn't judge me; they seemed to *want* to be around me. That surprised me a little, but I don't suppose it should have. Nashville is mainly an entertainment-town, and in entertainment, unfortunately, sexual misbehavior is fairly common. Even having an affair isn't an *unpardonable* sin; it's one that people just don't talk about.

"You got a raw deal," people would say to me about Warner Alliance dropping me. For a long time, I thought I got a raw deal too. I was angry that Christian stores around the country were returning my records, that the William Morris Agency had canceled all my dates, that one day I could get anyone I wanted on the phone and the next no one would return my calls. I was angry that when I considered my marriage a failure, I was both too stupid to hang tough and too weak to ignore Norman and seek a divorce. Instead, I had used Marabeth's pregnancy to get out of it in the most spectacular and damaging way possible.

Still, I felt rejected by the industry I'd called home, and remembering the Scriptures that say Christians should help a brother when he's down, I also felt persecuted. I had committed adultery, not murder, I thought. It was easier to count the ways I felt Christian music had mistreated me than the ways I could have behaved differently. It was more satisfying to feel angry than ashamed. So when the Nashville party circuit embraced me and sympathized with me, I felt vindicated.

And that's how it happened that a Christian singer with long hair, earrings, money, and an attitude arrived thirsty in the "Promised Land" of women, liquor, and 24/7 praise.

"I think you did the right thing, Michael," people would tell me in smoky lounges over Cape Codders and Long Island iced teas.

"You got screwed, Michael."

"I love your music, Michael."

"Here's my number, Michael. Call me."

It was just what my itching ears wanted to hear. You have to realize that the whole night-life scene was 100 percent new to me. Being booked to sing gospel almost every weekend since I was a kid, I had never spent time in clubs. And I didn't have much experience with women, having had only a couple of serious girlfriends before I got married at age twenty. I'd also been raised to believe that all drinkers were bad people, and I despised alcohol, especially the smell. So the Nashville club scene was exciting and different at first, and I started meeting a whole new crowd, nice people who drank and danced and partied late into the night and seemed to be having a great time doing it. People who didn't care what I'd done. I didn't know whether it was my appearance or my notoriety, but I enjoyed the fact that when I walked into a room, people looked. My friends and I always got the best tables, the best food, the VIP treatment. Missy tells people today, "It was like going out to clubs with a rock star."

I never went out at night without a "posse." At the time, I guess it made me look popular, but the truth was, I had this idea that anyone who went to a nightclub alone was some kind of pathetic loser. And because I always—*always*—picked up the tab, I was never alone. Night after night, I racked up $400 bar tabs and didn't think twice if it topped out at a thousand. And I *fought* to pay the check. No matter how many times I'd played to sellout crowds, heard fans calling out my name, seen girls fighting to get to me or people clamoring to get my autograph, I still felt like the uncool guy in the room. I had no confidence that anyone liked me for me. If I kept picking up the tab, I reasoned, at least I'd always have someone around.

That was one reason I started to make a regular habit of popping a Loritab before I went clubbing. Just one pill turned me into a new man. There was the timid, sober Michael and the high, outgoing Michael. I liked that second guy and wanted to be him, not that other Michael English who had grown up shy and backward. I didn't think it was any big deal. The pills just loosened me up. Besides, they were legal.

But I had another reason for dabbling in pills. As I had learned when I had the flu, painkillers dissolved more than just physical pain; they also numbed me to the pain of regret. One dose and for a few hours I didn't think about my failed marriage, about living apart from my daughter, about my ruined career, or about the shame that gnawed at me when I wasn't quick enough to blot it out with anger. One pill and a warm, carefree glow replaced all that, as though nothing in life mattered but the present.

+ chapter twenty-nine +

Soon I was in complete rebellion. Not so much against God Himself, but against the Whole Christian Thing. It was fake, I had decided. Christians loved you when you were up and kicked you when you were down. I came to believe that my party friends were much more authentic. When they got a few drinks in them, they'd *really* tell you what they thought. I had hated drinking since the days of checking under Mama's vanity, but I started to indulge a little. Then a little more. Before long, Missy was driving me home, often having to pull over to the side of the road so I could lean out of the car and puke in the gutter.

For a long time, I looked at the pills as a weekend thing, the way other guys look at drinking. But I soon began stretching out that excuse and bracketing every day between Thursday and Sunday under the heading "weekend." Gradually, I started to find more and more occasions that deserved a pill. Taking a woman to dinner? Pop a pill. Good game on TV? Pop a pill.

One weekend I house-sat for a friend. She had a very nice condo, and I invited Missy and some other characters I'd met over to cook out and watch Michael Jordan and the Chicago Bulls in the NBA finals. I vividly remember how, as we got the food ready, I looked forward to taking my first Loritab. And I remember sitting on the couch in front of the game smiling, my eyelids just slightly heavy like a cat in the sun, my legs dissolving into noodles, thinking, *Man, it doesn't get any better than this.*

the prodigal comes home

Looking back, it's sad to think that was my big moment. That such an empty, lonely thrill was what I looked forward to most. Missy could see the road I was headed down, and every once in a while she'd say something to me about taking too many pills. She also confided in her parents.

Missy is really close to her dad, Topper, the pastor, and her mom, whose real given name is Glorious. (I've always thought those were great names.) And since Missy and I were forever going out, getting ready to go out, or coming home from being out, she was often with me when she called home to check in with her folks. Most times she'd talk to them for a while, then hold out the phone. "Here. Dad wants to talk to you."

I'd roll my eyes and hold the phone up to my head, but not too close. "Mikey, buddy, let me pray for you real quick," Topper would say. He always called me Mikey, and he always prayed a short little prayer like, "Lord, we know You love Mikey, that he's Your child, and that You're not through with him yet. Just help Mikey through this time, Lord. In Jesus's name. Amen."

And that was it. Topper didn't tell me to quit drinking or partying. He didn't tell me I'd better get myself back to church. He just told me God loved me. And for about four years, the Reverend Topper Council of Paducah, Kentucky, was the only minister who would tell me that. I didn't want to hear it, but Topper told me anyway.

In 1996 Curb released my second pop solo album, *Freedom.* A song from that record, "Your Love Amazes Me," really broke me into the pop world. A nationally syndicated deejay, Delilah, started playing it on the radio, and soon the song made it to number five on the Adult Contemporary chart. As it climbed in the rankings, I remember listening to Dick Clark's American Top 40 on Sunday mornings.

"Here's song number five this week from newcomer Michael English . . ." It was the coolest thing hearing Dick Clark say my name. As bad as it sounds, I had an attitude like, *I'm going to be a huge pop star. And all those Christian so-and-sos who threw me out—I'll show them.* But as much as I tried to pretend to be happy about the relative success of *Freedom,* my heart wasn't in it. I missed gospel music—and I hated that I missed it. Whenever I came across any Christian music on television or on the radio, I felt a stab of regret. It was like catching a glimpse of a true love that you let slip away. When you're singing a gospel song, there's a reason for it. You're sending out a message. Pop music, to me, was just singing a song. And it wasn't until I had stepped over from one music world into the other that I realized for the first time how much I really meant that message.

A Christian song always took me to a place where nothing else—not a church service, not a sermon, not a prayer—could take me. But for most of my life, gospel music had been tied up with business to some extent. It was not until I left it that I realized that it was much more than business. Singing was my worship. No matter how shallow my faith was, no matter how much I struggled with Scripture, I was closest to God when I sang a gospel song. I had struggled for so long in my faith that gospel music had become my only tie to God. And now it was gone.

Pop success didn't make me happy, because my heart was turned toward home, toward Christian music. I just wanted to be back there, singing and performing, hanging out with those people I'd known for so long as my friends. It wasn't that I wanted to be a big star again. I would have been happy just to participate. All I wanted was to belong.

+ chapter thirty +

After trying for years to crash my way out of my marriage to Lisa, I was surprised to find that I couldn't stand to be alone. And I couldn't just date. I fell into a series of relationships, some of them positive, such as the one with Beth, a pretty retail manager in her early twenties who really was what you would call a good girl from a terrific family. But I couldn't be satisfied.

While shooting the video for "Love Moves in Mysterious Ways," I met Jennifer Rand, a strikingly beautiful model. The director had given me headshots of several girls who could play my love interest in the video. She was exotic-looking with high cheekbones, a full mouth, and wide eyes tilted up at the corners. And because of her features, she could get away with wearing her hair so short that it was nearly a crew cut. The director encouraged me to choose her; he thought the unusual contrast—a man with long hair and a woman with short hair—would make the video visually interesting. Jennifer and I hit it off on the set and steamed up the video, and before I knew it, she was keeping two drawers of clothing in my apartment. I had moved out of Larry and Naomi's condo and rented a place in Bellevue. Jennifer and I half lived together. She was a tree-hugging, tie-dyed free spirit who wore vintage clothes, and I was crazy about her. She had an independent attitude that said, *I'm going to do what I want to do, and if you don't like it, too bad.* Eventually that included being with another man, which pretty much ended our relationship. How's that for reaping what you've sown?

the prodigal comes home

AFTER JENNIFER LEFT, I added a new activity to my Things I've Never Done Before list: I started going to strip clubs. Why? Because I knew it was wrong. What did it matter? I figured I was headed to hell anyway, and partying a little heartier wasn't going to make it any hotter. Over time, I developed an attitude that said, *If I'm going to have the bad-boy reputation, then fine: I'll be bad.*

My favorite spot in Nashville was Ken's Gold Club. You couldn't buy liquor there, but the dancers stripped completely naked inches from the customers. One of them, a girl named Tina, blew my mind. She was stunning—and not just when the lights were low. She could have been a model or an actress. I couldn't believe she was working as a stripper.

A few weeks after I first spotted Tina at Ken's, I saw her again at a cocktail party at Trilogy, a new restaurant that Naomi and Larry had opened. When I turned around, there she was, on the arm of a much older man. When I noticed the man excuse himself, I walked over and smiled down at her. "Do I know you?" I asked.

She smiled her knockout smile. "Yeah. I work at Ken's Gold Club."

I nodded toward her date, who was standing at the bar. "Is that your boyfriend?"

"No, I'm his escort. He paid me five hundred dollars to be seen here with him."

At that moment, I should have said, "Well, it was nice meeting you. Good night." Instead, I asked, "Well, what does it take for a guy like me to go out with a girl like you?"

She smiled again. "A pen."

The night I wrote down her number was the beginning of a turbulent relationship. Tina was only nineteen. She told me horrible stories about her upbringing that I can't repeat here. Let it be enough to say that I wasn't surprised anymore that she'd wound up stripping. Tina moved in with me. At that point I decided that I didn't want anyone else watching her dance. We fought and fought over it, but she made a lot of money at it and wouldn't give it up.

During all this time, Megan and I still saw each other regularly, and she thought all my girlfriends hung the moon and wanted to be just like them. Lisa wasn't thrilled about that, but she never tried to keep Megan away from me, and she never talked me down to her, even when I tried to be the cool dad by taking Megan to do things her mom wouldn't let her do, like get a piercing way up high on her ear. (Lisa had a fit about that.)

But as I descended deeper into the Nashville nightlife, I began to do things that definitely weren't cool, like showing up drunk or high in front of Megan. Among the things that I'll always regret are the times when she worried for me.

"Daddy, you drink too much," she'd say, not knowing about the pills. "Will you stop drinking, Daddy? Please?"

I promised her that I would. But, of course, I didn't.

Meanwhile, Tina started hanging around with Kelly, a girl I thought was bad news. After a year of screaming matches, insane jealousy, and what turned out to be secret phone calls, we broke it off. But that didn't keep me from winding up in the headlines again.

Tina and I were like gasoline and a match. On May 31, 1996, Missy and I had gone out with my road manager, Scott Wilemon, and a good friend Louis Upkins, to a nightclub called Soul Satisfaction. I hadn't taken any pills that night, but I'd smoked some pot and drunk some wine. We'd been standing in line just talking, when I turned around and spotted Tina and Kelly. I can't even remember who said what first, but we started in on each other, screaming and cussing in front of a crowd.

My friends got between us and talked me into leaving. We drove back to my apartment, with me griping and cursing about Tina and Kelly the whole way. To drown out the night, I swallowed a bunch of Percoset, a painkiller, and got dangerously stoned. Scott and Missy spent the night at my place—separately, of course—and the next morning, when Missy opened the door to leave, she found every news outlet in Nashville clustered on the front porch.

As it turned out, after Tina left Soul Satisfaction the night before, she went straight to the police. And somehow, between the club and the precinct, our verbal altercation turned into assault and theft. Tina told the police that I hit her at the club and that I refused to give her back some belongings she'd kept at my house. She filed formal charges against me, with Kelly as her witness. By the time I woke up that morning, reporters were all over it.

the prodigal comes home

The next day, the police came looking for me. My attorney advised me that it would be best, especially since I was innocent, to cooperate and turn myself in. When I did, the police booked me and snapped my mug shot, which, of course, the local news programs promptly broadcast on TV. It didn't matter that I hadn't done anything.

Weeks passed as speculation swirled in the music industry, and, I was later told, among Nashville's Christian community, that Michael English had really gone all the way down the toilet this time. Arrested. Booked. Even had his mug shot on the news. The coverage and the gossip weren't nearly as flashy, though, when not long afterward, Tina dropped the charges. My attorney, Rose Palermo, captured her on tape talking with Kelly about how they had made the whole thing up. But from the standpoint of reputation, it was too late. This was strike two in the eyes of many people: First, the affair. Now an assault charge. Sure, the charge was dropped, but the incident left lingering doubts in many people's minds—had I really assaulted her and gotten off easy?

Strike three came soon afterward. On August 27, 1996, while on my way home from the Nashville airport, the police pulled me over for speeding. I opened my glove compartment, where I kept my registration, having forgotten that was where I also sometimes kept a loaded gun.

"Sir, don't move!" the officer said. "Get out of the car and put your hands where I can see them!"

Another officer handcuffed me as his partner searched my car and found several bottles of prescription painkillers. I was high on them, but they couldn't tell. And they couldn't arrest me for the bottles since my name was on them. But I could hear them making cracks that I was another Christian hypocrite. The cops cited me for the gun, which was unregistered, and drove off with it. Later in court, my lawyer intervened and I got off with a fine. But once again, I made the news.

If I hadn't been the prodigal of Christian music already, I was now. I had become the black sheep, the jailbird relative families like to pretend they don't have. I learned later that when industry people read about the gun charge coming right on the heels of the assault charge, that was about the time many of them wished I would just go away.

+ chapter thirty-one +

In late '96 or early '97, Mark Lowry brought a talented bass player named Jay DeMarcus to one of my concerts. I had known Jay in Christian music. He'd had a band called East to West, but they'd split up. It was perfect timing. My road manager, Scott, had just moved back home to Mississippi. I needed some help, and Jay needed work. We hooked up and made a great team. He helped me put a smoking band together and also added a huge dose of fun to my stage show. Jay could do a hilarious, dead-on imitation of me, and we worked it in as a sort of straight man-funny man comedy act. Onstage, he would go to the mike, lower his chin, look up with his eyes, and say very seriously, "I believe . . . in a place called Hope. . . ."

I'd stand off to the side and shake my head, "embarrassed." The crowds ate it up. One night we did a concert at Lee University, Jay's alma mater, in Cleveland, Tennessee. We were singing with a choir, and the venue was packed. Jay knew I always kept four bottles of water onstage and sipped from them throughout the show. That night, after we finished the first song, I grabbed a bottle, turned it up, and immediately spewed a huge mouthful of clear liquid all over the stage. Jay almost fell over laughing, and the audience roared. He had filled all four water bottles with straight vodka.

By then I owed Curb a new album. I was ecstatic when they agreed to let me go back to my Southern gospel roots and record some old favorites. I chose songs I'd been singing my whole life, like "Blessed Assurance" and "Dig a Little Deeper." But I added a bluesy, New Orleans flavor to them— "put a little English on 'em," as they say. Jay and I produced the record, and his cousin Gary LeVox sang background vocals. We debuted *Gospel* on the Trinity Broadcasting Network, and it became one of my best-selling records.

I had performed on TBN before, and the network founders, Paul and Jan Crouch, loved my music. In mid-1998 they offered me my own program, *The Michael English Show*, with a kind of talk-show format where guests would perform, then I'd interview them. I had Christian artists on, like the Martins and Selah. Missy's dad, Topper, did a show. Once Mama came on and did a country cooking show where she whipped up creamed corn, butterbeans, and macaroni and tomatoes. We had a great time.

I also performed on the show, and Jay and the band would play for me. Down the line, Jay and his cousin Gary would finally get a big break of their own. They played a couple of nights a week at a live-music bar called Fiddle and Steel. Some industry scouts heard them there and offered them a recording contract. And a couple of years later, Jay and Gary launched a little country group called Rascal Flatts.

IT'S A CLICHÉ AS OLD AS THE HILLS, but God moves in mysterious ways, weaving together people's lives like a tapestry. We can only see the few threads that form our own lives, but looking down from heaven, He can see the big picture. In 1998 I met three women; two would figure into my life in important ways, and one would change me forever.

I met Jackie McCall at a concert I did in Ohio, where she lived. She was a pretty, down-to-earth girl, and we dated on and off, keeping in touch by phone. I liked Jackie a lot and was crazy about her parents, Lloyd and Verna. They took to me too, and I visited them whenever I could.

While performing in Cleveland, Tennessee, I met Gina, a nice girl from a good family. She and I began a serious relationship, and eventually she moved in with me. Gina was with me in December 1998 when I met Marcie Stambaugh, a young woman from Lansing, Michigan.

Marcie was a "PK"—a pastor's kid. The family came from a conservative

Brethren background. Her older brother, Chad, walked the straight and narrow, and her older sister, Katie, was downright angelic. Marcie says she used to call Katie "Little Miss Perfect"-PK and proud of it.

Marcie was the rebel in the family. Her mother, Cindy, was a cheerful, affectionate, soft-spoken woman. Her dad, Michael, was a pastor in a Brethren church. He was conservative, strict, and sold out to the church. The church was his life and so many times that left his family on the back burner, including his wife and children.

When Marcie was six years old, her mother experienced a moral failure which eventually led her parents to divorce. Her dad resigned his pastorate and took a job as an associate pastor in nearby Holt. But he too failed morally, resigned from the church, and took a job in construction.

Marcie's life turned upside down. Her family had gone from living a middle-class suburban life to eviction by default. Her father couldn't pay the bills, and the kids went to live with their mother. That marked the beginning of Marcie's rebellion.

She felt that both of her parents had betrayed the Christian values they claimed to believe in. Did they think living God's way wasn't worth the trouble? Marcie began to question whether God was really as powerful and loving as they had taught her. God hadn't done anything for her family, Marcie felt, so why should she bother with Him?

She got into a couple of unhealthy relationships and also experimented with alcohol and drugs. Still, she knew there was a calling on her life. "I fought God so hard," she told me after we met. "The minute I was sober, I could feel God calling me."

She fought Him until January 1998. Then she drove to her father's new home in Cadillac, Michigan. Her father had since repented and turned back to Christ. By this time, some six years later, He had remarried and was serving again as an associate pastor. Marcie shared with him about her longing for God, but she felt she was too far gone, had sinned too much.

"Look at my life, Marcie," her dad told her, "none of us is ever too far away from God for Him to forgive and accept." That's when Marcie realized that God hadn't failed her family after all. And shortly after, she placed her trust in Christ.

the prodigal comes home

Marcie had grown up listening to Southern gospel and inspirational music and had heard mine without really knowing it was me. Her dad loved the Cathedrals and the Gaithers and had played that kind of music at home all the time. Later her sister played Gospel in her car. When Marcie heard "I Bowed on My Knees," she cried.

After so much rebellion in her teen years, the lyrics "I want to see Jesus because He's the One who died for me" flooded her heart with relief and joy. It wasn't my singing. As I said before, it's just that kind of song.

Katie had gotten the tape from Marcie's friend Melissa, who owned every solo album I'd made. In December 1998, Melissa invited Marcie to come with her to see me in concert. Melissa had played radio songs like "In Christ Alone" and "Mary, Did You Know?" for Marcie, but she'd never really made the connection between those and the songs from *Gospel*. When she found out that Michael English sang them both, she was excited about the concert.

On the way to the concert, Melissa filled her in on the gory details: the affair with Marabeth, the public fall from grace, my attempts to start singing Christian music again.

"I remember thinking, here's someone who has a story kind of like mine," she told me later. "I'm from a screwed-up family, and he sounds like he's kind of screwed up too." She thought that was refreshing because she'd spent most of her life around really solid Christians.

"Nobody I knew had a past like me," she said. "So it was refreshing to see someone fall and come back."

Of course, she didn't know that I hadn't really come back. I may have been singing Christian music again, but I wasn't living a Christian life. I knew that and was careful with my testimony in concert. When I would talk to audiences, I would talk about repentance and struggle and seeking God. I'm sure they all assumed I was talking only about the past, about the affair with Marabeth. But I was also talking about my growing battle with drugs.

Some might read that and think it was just more hypocrisy. And maybe it was. I guess the question is whether I should have stopped singing praise to God because I was sinning. Should I have stopped doing what God made me to do because I wasn't living a perfect life? Should a Christian architect who's cheating on his wife stop building skyscrapers? The argument can be made that singing Christian music is a ministry, that I was speaking for and somehow representing God. I wonder whether that doesn't place Christian singers on too high a pedestal. Yes, it is a ministry; we are role models whether we like it or not and should live by the message of our music. But we also have to pay the rent. Singing is also a job, like running a company or driving a bus. If everyone who sinned had to stop going to church and doing "Christian" things, every church in America would shut down.

I'm not arguing that people in public ministry ought to be able to engage in habitual sin and keep ministering. But I am saying that Christians in ministry struggle just like everyone else. "Public" Christians can repent—then slide back into sin and struggle some more. In the war between the spirit and the flesh, as the writer of Hebrews says, we are easily entangled. I wasn't always repentant during those years. But during much of that time, I burned with Paul's dilemma in Romans 7: "What I do is not the good I want to do; no, the evil I do not want to do—this I keep on doing. . . . What a wretched man I am! Who will rescue me from this body of death?"

I didn't get onstage and holler Paul's famous words into the microphone, but I did try to be open about the fact that I was still struggling just like everyone else and that God is a merciful Father who forgives us.

That was the message Marcie heard when she came to hear me at Michigan State University in December 1998. Looking back on it, knowing what she knows now, she tells me, "I could tell you didn't want to lie, but you couldn't tell the truth, . . . that you were just trying every day to be the man God wanted you to be."

She also says now that there was one thing I said that made her feel I was speaking directly to her that night: "This burden you're carrying around, these sins you've committed—you have to know that you're forgiven."

Melissa, Marcie, and another friend, Lindsay, came up onstage afterward. Someone snapped a photo of them with me.

"Your story was amazing," Marcie told me. "It really touched me."

"Thank you," I said.

I couldn't help noticing how pretty she was, like Marissa Tomei, Jenna Elfman, and Ashley Judd all rolled into one. But there were other people in line to meet me, so I turned away to greet the next person, and that was that. I didn't know it at the time, but Marcie would pray for me for the next three years. She didn't buy my records, and she didn't follow my career. Instead, she just prayed from afar that God would bless my ministry. Even more fervently, she prayed that He would also take away this nagging, ridiculous, outrageous feeling she had that she was supposed to marry me.

+ chapter thirty-two +

Gina and I continued our relationship, and over the next year, I slipped further into the grip of painkillers. By then, taking pills had ceased to be a willful thing; it was more like quicksand sucking me down. I went from taking one pill before clubbing on Saturday night to taking one on both Friday and Saturday night, then Thursday through Saturday, until before I knew it, I was taking pills three times a day, every day.

I continued to see Megan, but I became an unreliable dad. She was a teenager by then, and when she came to stay over at my apartment, I'd sometimes leave her there and go clubbing. Hours later she'd call my cell phone.

"Daddy, when are you coming home?"

"I'm going to leave here in just a few minutes, baby," I'd shout into the phone over the club music. And two hours later my little girl would have to call me again.

As my pill taking got worse, Megan couldn't count on me at all. I would tell her I was coming to a dance recital, and she would wait for me, but I would never come. It still turns my stomach to think of the times when I was high, or drunk, or both, and I'd get depressed. I'd lay my head on Megan's shoulder, and she'd comfort me. Again, she took care of me when I should have been taking care of her.

Those kinds of scenes made me realize that pills were no longer a recreational drug. They had become a permanent part of my life. And before long, I had a new realization: pills *were* my life. Somehow, though, I kept making and performing music. In 1999 I recorded *Heaven to Earth*, my first real attempt to reenter contemporary Christian music.

By then I had a $400-a-day pill habit, $25 for every hour I was awake. And most of those hours I spent swallowing pills, counting pills, or scheming how I would get more pills. I used a *Physician's Desk Reference* to make sure the pills I bought were the real thing. I bought them from street dealers. I bought them from old people who supplemented their social security checks by selling prescriptions they didn't need. I "doctor shopped," making the rounds of medical clinics and exaggerating pain symptoms to get my own prescriptions. I even got pills from Cathy, a Texas nurse who worked in a doctor's office. She offered to "borrow" pills from her boss's supply and send them to me in the mail. Of course, I accepted.

Taking painkillers became less and less about getting a buzz and more and more about taking enough hydrocodone to ward off withdrawals. I became an expert; I knew exactly how many of which kind of pill I had to take to make myself feel sane again. I was searching for something to fill a hole inside me, one that had always been there. At first the hole had been the size of a pinprick, but it had continued to get bigger and bigger without my even knowing it. And the more pills I took, the larger the hole became.

I *hated* the craving. I hated being a slave to addiction. At times I got on my knees and begged God to change me, but then I couldn't get up from my knees and go make the change. I found myself sobbing when there was no one else in the house. In the shower I'd slowly stop washing and just stand with my face pointed up, weeping uncontrollably, the spray raining down hot grief instead of water. Sometimes I would sit down on the hard tile, hold my knees, and rock back and forth, back and forth, crying out to God, "Where *are* You? Why can't You show Your face to me just once and let me know it's going to be okay?"

I was always screaming for a sign. But the next minute, I'd tell myself, *You know what? God doesn't care about you, so screw it.* And I would turn back to my new god, chemical escape.

For months Gina struggled as she watched me losing my internal tug-of-war and sliding deeper into the pit of addiction. I repeatedly told her how much I wanted to be free of the painkillers, and one day I talked about somehow weaning myself off them. That gave her an idea. She said she knew a Cleveland, Tennessee, doctor who had once weaned himself off cocaine using a step-down method that was supposed to prevent withdrawals.

"Maybe he could help," she said.

Gina knew about how Dr. Robert Nathan had kicked his long-ago coke habit because she had once dated his son. She called ahead, and he agreed to see me. That same week, we drove the two and a half hours to Cleveland to see him at his small-town family practice.

I'm not sure why Dr. Nathan agreed to try to help me. Maybe he saw my desperation. When we sat down with him in his small, plain office, I was as honest with him as I could be. I told him what I was taking and how much.

"How bad am I?" I asked him, hoping his answer would motivate me even more to get off the pills.

"You're as bad as you can get without moving over to something else," Dr. Nathan said. By that he meant heroin.

Then he explained his plan for treating me. He would write prescriptions for the drugs I was addicted to, and I would take them according to a schedule. I can't remember the dosages exactly, but the idea was this: For one week, I would take four Loritabs in the morning, afternoon, and evening. The next week, I would take four in the morning, three in the afternoon, and four at night. Then the week after that, the dose would be four, three, and three. That's how slow I was going to do this—and if I was faithful, I could kick the addiction without going through withdrawals.

I knew plenty about withdrawals, and the thought of that torture terrified me. I knew that the compressed timeline, sweat, nausea, and pain they showed in the movies was nothing compared to the true agony of beating hydrocodone. Oxycontin, the version I was addicted to, is so powerful it was originally manufactured for cancer patients to help them through their last excruciating weeks or months of pain before death. Detox wards all over the country have as many Oxy addicts as those hooked on heroin or crack. If more people understood that, they'd never touch painkillers in the first place.

When Dr. Nathan told me his plan, I began to get excited. *I'm going to get off this stuff,* I thought. *I'm under a doctor's care. . . . I'm going to get my life back!*

Elated and encouraged, Gina and I drove back to Nashville, and I started following Dr. Nathan's schedule. Gina's job was to hold the pills and give them to me as he had ordered. That didn't last long. I quickly found that Dr. Nathan's step-down method robbed me of the "high" I craved. After a week, I began finding excuses—a headache or a fight with Lisa—for taking more pills than I was supposed to. It was easy to use my junkie charm to manipulate Gina into giving me a little extra.

"I'll take two less tomorrow," I'd promise. When she tried to protest or hold the line, I'd whine or sulk or yell at her to give me the pills or get out.

Finally, Gina couldn't take it anymore, and she did get out—out of my life. And the Cleveland plan became just one more way to get more drugs.

I began experimenting to learn how I could maximize the effect of different pills. I'd take them on an empty stomach or take them with liquor. I still hated alcohol, still despised the smell and the taste, but I would do anything to intensify the effect of the pills, so I drank.

I also scoured books, researching what kind of pills could deliver the most hydrocodone with the least "buffer," which was usually aspirin or acetaminophen. Too much analgesic made me nauseous, in part because it was systematically destroying my liver.

To finance my habit, I began selling my clothes and other belongings on eBay. I would advertise them as "Michael English's clothes," selling the expensive shirts and jackets I'd worn onstage over the years. I sold a Warner Alliance jacket, a collector's item I cherished. It was only Missy's angry protest that kept me from selling the framed, autographed hankie that Vestal Goodman had given me. At the time, sentimental value was nothing compared with my craving for narcotics.

There were a few times when money and timing coincided in such a way that I was able to score three or four hundred pills all at once. And when I did, I would rush home, lock the front door, hurry back to my bedroom, and pour them all onto the bed like treasure. I emptied out all the bottles and little packets and mixed the tablets together in one big pile, swirling and sifting the blue Loritabs, cream Oxycontins, yellow Norcos, beige Percosets, even the little light green ones I didn't like. *Beautiful.* There in my room, I played with the pills, running my hands through the colors like a thief after a jewel heist, glorying in the fact that I had such a huge supply.

I'm going to be happy for a while now, I thought.

And for that one day, I would be. I'd plan out a really good day, have people over, laugh some. Those were dangerous times. I had hundreds of pills and could take as many as I wanted. I sometimes took handfuls. In fact, the more pills I had, the less time they lasted. Within two days of a big score, I'd begin to worry again where I was going to get more. By the third day, I would begin to ration. I could never let down my guard, because I never had enough pills. Never.

+ chapter thirty-three**+**

By 2000 I had been a full-blown addict for nearly two years. The focus of my life had narrowed to a pinpoint: pills. Getting enough of them into my body every few hours to keep myself alive. I had become a grungy, unwashed hermit. My weight ballooned to two hundred seventy-five pounds. I didn't wash my clothes. I rarely bathed. Pumpkin, the poodle, had gone to live with Lisa and Megan, but I had two new dogs, a miniature schnauzer named Gracie, and Kramer, a toy poodle. I rarely mustered up the energy to take them outside. My apartment began to stink.

Finally, Missy and I had a horrible fight. She was sick to death of watching me destroy myself, she said. She went back to Paducah to help take care of her grandfather, who was ill. Jay's Rascal Flatts project was taking off, so we didn't talk much anymore. I would have felt utterly and completely alone except for one thing: I had become certain I was being watched.

It began one evening in January when the phone rang. I was running low on pills and had been trying to get more from Cleveland. Hopefully, I picked up the cordless receiver and punched the talk button. "Hello?"

Silence on an open line.

"Hello?" I said again. I thought I heard clicking and quickly hung up. Paranoia spread through my bones like winter.

The calls continued for a few days, and I became so paranoid that I wouldn't go outside. I bolted the front door and snapped the blinds shut tight, hoping to disappear behind the thin plastic. Still, I felt so nervous and unsettled that I kept creeping back to check them both. I didn't dare take the dogs out, fearing that police had staked out my place and were hiding outside in the bushes just waiting to jump out and arrest me. So Gracie and Kramer did their business in the house, leaving little piles on the carpet. With Missy gone, the stink in the apartment grew worse.

At one point, I called Cathy in Dallas. We talked about when she could send me more pills, but in semicode. "I think my phone is bugged," I told her, half whispering. "Gotta go. Bye." I hung up.

Suddenly four hard knocks rattled the front door. My heart froze. The dogs went nuts, yapping and barking, but I didn't dare shush them. Thoughts raced through my brain: *Those were loud knocks! Not casual . . . not friendly . . . not a neighbor.*

My heart pounded in my chest. I glanced at the blinds. Did they cover all the cracks? Could anyone possibly see me moving around inside? I didn't think so. I edged over to the door on Indian feet and put my eye to the peephole. I held my breath as if whoever was outside might hear me breathing.

Through the fish-eye lens, I could see two middle-aged men. I had never seen them before in my life. Cops? Maybe. Probably. Fear squeezed my chest. I decided to play possum until they went away.

Rap-rap-rap! The knocking came right in my face, and I jerked my head back, shocked. Panic set in, and my breaths came short and quick. Suddenly I was sure the men outside were the law. Only cops banged on a door that way—the way that says, "Come out! We know you're in there!"

Like a thief in my own house, I backed silently away from the door and sat down on the couch to wait them out. My heart was now galloping like a runaway horse. I imagined that the strangers on my porch had their ears pressed to the door and could hear it. Time passed . . . five minutes, fifteen, thirty. When I felt I had waited long enough, I crept back to the door and put my eye to the peephole again.

The men were gone.

That night I tore through my medicine cabinet and stripped out all my empty pill bottles in case of a police raid. I stuffed the bottles into my kitchen trash. I found a few tablets of Mepergan, a painkiller I didn't like, and threw those away too. Strangely, I also began to obsess about taking the dogs out. It wasn't like I hadn't gone days without doing so before. In a way, I was like a man playing Russian roulette who hopes he will live but secretly has a death wish. Maybe I consciously hoped to remain free but secretly wanted to be caught. Whatever psychology applies, I waited until nearly midnight, then leashed the dogs and slowly, carefully opened the door.

+ chapter thirty-four +

Nothing. No one.

I swiveled my head back and forth, scanning the empty breezeway. I edged up to the railing and checked the dark complex grounds, the lamp-lit parking areas, the street. Nothing seemed suspicious. *Maybe I'm just being paranoid.* Raring to go, Gracie and Kramer pulled me toward the stairs. I took them down, hurried them in the grass, and made it back to the apartment, relieved that I hadn't acquired any handcuffs along the way.

The next day I was down to four Oxycontins. In terms of supply, that was red alert status, but the Cleveland doctor had given me some pain patches, sort of like the ones smokers use to step down their nicotine intake. I slapped on two patches and phoned a friend in Cleveland, who said he'd drive in with my prescription the following day. Satisfied that I'd soon have a fresh round of pills, I swallowed my last Oxys that night about seven o'clock and settled in to watch TV.

Rap-rap-rap!

Gracie and Kramer went crazy again, and my stomach fell away as if I were strapped into one of those free-fall rides at Six Flags. The blinds were still closed tight. I stood and walked quietly to the fish-eye lens. The same men stood outside, their faces glowing yellow in the porch light.

Who are *they?* I wondered. *If they are police,* I reasoned, *wouldn't they have staked out the place last night and got me when I went out to walk the dogs? Maybe it's nothing.* I decided to take my chances and opened the door.

"Mr. English?" said a graying, balding man wearing a Tennessee Titans T-shirt.

"Yes?"

He held up his badge. "We have a warrant to search the premises for narcotics."

I can't explain the fear that engulfed me. I'd been in trouble before, with the gun charge and the nightclub incident. But this was the real deal. This was going-to-prison fear. Lose-my-freedom fear. In a dark, devastating instant, I was certain that my life was over.

Four men pushed past me, the two middle-aged men and two bruisers, bodyguard types. All wore plain clothes.

"I need you to take your animals and put them in the bathroom," Titans said.

He was curt, businesslike. I did what he said, then returned to sit on the couch. The bruisers headed back to the bedroom to begin their search. From the living room, I could hear the sound of drawers opening, clothes sliding on the closet rail, things falling from boxes. Titans and the other detective, a big man himself, began to rifle through my kitchen, starting with the trash. Titans upended the kitchen trash can over the stovetop, and a small cascade of pill bottles, along with the Mepergan, came tumbling out. I had been smart enough to clean out my medicine cabinet but too stupid to take out the trash.

"Well, look what we got here," Big Man said. "Tried to get rid of it, didn't he?"

I looked away, my legs moving, shaking. Images of an ugly future bloomed in my head like nightmares. *Everyone will know I'm an addict. What about the new record,* Heaven to Earth? *My "Christian comeback" will debut just as I'm going to prison. . . . Dear God, Megan will have to come see her daddy in prison.*

Big Man walked over and showed me his open palm where three pills lay. "What are these?"

"Mepergan," I said. "They're painkillers. I can't take them. They knock me out."

Over in the kitchen, Titans had found my *Physician's Desk Reference* and another pill book on top of a kitchen cabinet. The newspapers would later say the police found blank prescription pads, which was a lie. I had broken the law, but hadn't sunk to forging prescriptions.

Then Titans came and sat next to me on the couch. "Mr. English, we have information that you have been obtaining prescriptions fraudulently. We've been listening to your phone conversations, and we had enough to indict you before we walked in here. Do you have anything else in the house?" He searched my eyes with his own.

I told him the truth. "If I had anything, I'd have taken it already."

The bruisers returned from the bedroom with a few odds and ends. Titans handed me a piece of paper, something legal, some official notice that I was a criminal suspect. Then they all walked out, pulling the door shut behind them. For a moment, relief rushed over me like a waterfall. I had expected to be led out in handcuffs, maybe with cameras rolling and neighbors watching, as Big Man shoved me into the back of a police cruiser with his hand on my head. But the relief faded quickly. In reality, I was still alone, sitting in a ransacked apartment, surrounded by dog crap, and probably on my way to prison.

+ chapter thirty-five +

Here's the mark of a hopeless addict: When the police raided my house, the thought of jail time terrified me. But the next day, being out of pills scared me even more. So when my Cleveland friend showed up with the prescription, I drove to a pharmacy and had it filled. If ever there was a sign that I had become an absolute and complete slave to narcotics, that was it. The police already knew about my Cleveland connection. They could have been tailing me and snatched away my freedom then and there. And I was such a junkie, I was willing to risk it.

I called Missy for help. She called my divorce attorney, Rose Palermo, who called me right away. "Michael, I have someone I want you to talk to. His name is David Raybin, and he's the best criminal attorney in town. He takes on a lot of high-profile cases."

It was going to be high-profile all right. I had been slowly working my way back into Christian music, and *Heaven to Earth* was set to release in weeks. I could already hear the television teaser: "Christian singer on comeback trail busted for narcotics. News at eleven."

Rose already had David Raybin holding on another line. She patched him in.

"First, Michael, everything's going to be okay," he said. "We're going to take care of this. All you have to do is listen to me and do exactly what I tell you to do."

David immediately made me feel better. He was a take-charge man but also encouraging. As we talked, I let him know I was willing to obey his instructions to the letter. Then he asked, "Are you still taking the pills?"

"I have to," I said. "I'm addicted."

"The first thing we need to do, then, is get you clean. Then we'll deal with the rest."

"Okay," I said. "Whatever I need to do."

The first thing I had to do was come up with some money to pay David. He cost $15,000 right off the bat. Not long before, I had learned I had an unused credit card with a huge credit limit. It was a good thing: it was all the money I had. And if I hadn't gotten in trouble when I did, I would have used it to get cash for drugs.

By that time I was no longer worried about my career. I knew I had dodged bullets—the gun charge, the false assault claim. At those times, I hadn't been all that concerned about serious consequences. This time was different, and it turned out to be even worse than I thought: David would later tell me that I faced up to twelve years in prison. The worst part was that even if I squeaked through with no jail time, I wouldn't come back to anything. Even though I had worked hard to shove my career back into drive, my secret addiction would ruin my return to Christian music. Not only that, but the most dreadful thing lay on the road between here and having nothing: the torture of getting off pills.

SEVEN DAYS AFTER MY ARREST, I climbed into a car with Missy Council and my business manager, Melanie Clark, and headed to the detox clinic at Vanderbilt University Hospital. All I carried with me was a duffel bag, my ball cap, and six Oxycontins, the last of my Cleveland prescription. I thought about hiding the pills in my hat, secret weapons against the pain I knew waited for me at the clinic. But I knew the clinic staff would search me, so I swallowed all six. They'd confiscate my last fix if they found it, but they couldn't confiscate it from my intestines.

Rolling through the Nashville night, I was scared of what lay ahead. I had read a lot about Oxycontin withdrawal, and it was supposed to be as bad as getting off heroin. But as scared as I was, I was also relieved. I was finally going to get off this stuff. I hated the fact that I had to live my life this way, scrounging, sneaking around in secret, dealing with the dregs of the world to try to buy more. I hated the awful secret I kept from my family. Most of all, I hated the way my addiction kept me from being a good father to Megan. All I wanted was life as it used to be, when I could wake up in the morning and not have to put pills in my mouth to survive.

As we neared the Vanderbilt hospital, I became aware of approaching a critical turning point, a make-or-break moment. I felt I would emerge from detox either a new man, ready to climb back into the driver's seat of my life, or a hopeless wreck, still flying down the road to self-destruction. If I had known what was coming within the next ninety-six hours, I might have jumped out of Missy's car and thrown myself off the nearest bridge.

We pulled up at Vanderbilt late at night, the sedan winding through streetlights and tree shadows. Melanie had suggested the late arrival as a way to cut the chances of a photo appearing in the next day's paper captioned "Michael English, arrested last week on drug charges, checks into detox." When we walked through the doors, the place seemed deserted except for a late-night skeleton crew and a few people in a place I learned later was called the "relaxation room." The nurse on duty was kind to me and explained what my schedule would be like for the next few days as I came off the drugs. With the six Oxys in me, I was able to listen to her as though I was sane.

Still, she confiscated my blow dryer, which had a long cord I could have used to hang myself, and also rifled through my toiletries looking for sharp things like nail files and hypodermic needles. Then she led me down a long, dim corridor to the last door on the right. The soft soles of her shoes whispered on the tile.

Another man was already in the room sleeping. I put down my duffel, crawled into bed with my clothes on, and slept on and off through the night. When morning came, thin stripes of weak sunlight slipped underneath the closed vertical blinds that covered the room's only window. In the dim light, I could see white walls, brown carpet, and a big, round classroom-style clock with black hands and numbers on a stark white face. The furniture was institutional oak.

the prodigal comes home

The first day passed as dull as the room. The other man had checked out early in the day, newly purified. He was the first person I saw at detox who was on the other side of what I was about to go through, and I wished I could be in his shoes. I hadn't changed into pajamas the night before, so I was still dressed in street clothes. For most of the morning, I stayed that way, lying on top of the covers with my ball cap pulled down over my eyes as though I were on vacation and napping by a lake instead of in a lockdown for junkies. Looking back on it, my body language must have screamed that I was not fully on board with this program.

The clinic rules demanded that I go down the hall to the nurses' station three times a day to have my vital signs checked. I did that but nothing else. A cafeteria was connected to the clinic, but I wasn't hungry. A relaxation room offered television and the company of others. I hated the thought of either.

Late that afternoon, a doctor in a white coat tapped on the door, then walked in. "How are you doing?" he asked.

"Okay right now," I said. "I'm a little anxious."

The doctor went out again and night came. That's when things started to go a little crazy.

+ chapter thirty-six +

I wasn't in pain—not yet. I felt this horrible combination of fear and desire. I knew what the feeling was, and I hated it. It was the same sensation I got at home when I ran out of pills. That's the part of addiction that nonusers probably don't understand: the anxiety over supply. I was used to taking pills as often as I wanted to—every three or four hours, or every thirty minutes if I felt like it. But if I didn't have pills left, I couldn't rest; I would obsess over getting more pills—*where* I was going to get more, and more important, *when* I was going to get them. Plotting and scheming ate me alive, and as it did, here came the anxiety, the crawling skin, my stomach suspended in the middle of a loop-the-loop stunt-plane ride, the need to be moving, always moving to hold off the pain in my legs. I couldn't even take a shower because the spray felt like needles on my skin.

It was weird, though: once I made a connection and was on my way to get more pills, my mind would talk me down. *You're on your way. In four hours you'll have more.* Just knowing I had a hookup relieved the creepy anxiety. I could deal with the symptoms then. Still, my stomach seemed to lift itself higher in my body and just hang there, suspended, as if I had already slipped over the big hill on a roller coaster and was screaming down the other side. And it stayed like that until I could swallow some more pills.

But here in the clinic, there would be no hookup, and my mind had a very different message for me: *It's just going to get worse from here.*

Day Two: I started getting cold. At intervals the doctor popped in.

"How are you doing? Do you need anything?" he asked.

"Not unless you can give me some Oxycontin." I didn't smile when I said it.

The only thing in detox that made me smile was the night nurse, Rita. The clinic nurses would make rounds, bringing blankets or just checking on me. But Rita, the late-night nurse, was special. A tall African-American woman with short hair, bright eyes, and a dazzling smile, she first came to my room on the second night.

"Michael, you're going to have to eat something," she said gently. "I know you're not hungry, but you're not going to get better if you don't get some food in your system." Rita brought me red Gatorade and laid a couple of saltine crackers on the desk that doubled as a nightstand. To me, she was like the Christian Jesus spoke of in the Gospel of Mark, bringing a cup of water in Jesus's name.

The other nurses would throw open the doors in the early dawn hours and bark out, "Vitals!" And shivering and dripping from withdrawals, patients were supposed to stagger down to the nurses' station and get checked at least once in the middle of the night. But Rita would see me writhing on the bed, barely staying sane, and would roll the vital-signs machine down to my room. When I think about her now, tears come. It wasn't her job to walk down there with that machine. The whole time I was there, she was like a ministering angel, a real example of Christian compassion. It helped so much, just the thought that somebody in there really cared. I hope she reads this so that she can know how much her kindness meant to me.

Day Three: Peak withdrawals set in. Sweat began pouring from every inch of my skin, soaking the sheets and the pillow. And yet I was freezing. Every time Rita checked on me, she brought another blanket. I writhed under the thick pile. It was night, pitch black in my room, with only the dim light from the hallway sliding up under the door. Every nerve ending in my body seemed alive with pain, as though each was a tiny blowtorch shooting razor-thin bursts of fire through my body. My skin crawled, my muscles cramped, my bones ached, and my guts gnawed as though my insides were eating their way to the surface. I wish I could truly tell you how *consuming* it was. Not one square inch of my body, not one hair follicle, not one eyelash was free of pain. It was as though pain were a jungle cat eating me alive— over and over and over again.

In the midst of the torture, the room mysteriously brightened and the pill rain started—that beautiful hail of Easter-colored tablets and caplets that fooled me into a few brief moments of hope. Looking back on that, I see how utterly pitiful it was, that my hope should be placed fully in those pills. I mean *fully*. They were my gods. As I lay in that bed certain that I was dying, I would have done almost anything to get even one of them. The hope I placed in them was as false as the hope we place in anything that isn't Christ. Desperation set in, and my junkie mind began to spin with schemes. *I've got to get out of here. Who can I call? Who'll come and get me?*

Mama.

Mama knew I was in here. When she found out the hell I was going through, she wouldn't be able to turn her back on me. She just didn't have it in her. When it was time to check vitals, I shuffled down the hall like an old man, meaning to stop at the pay phone I'd seen bolted to the hallway wall. As I walked, my clothing rubbed against me, causing every hair on my body to feel like a needle pivoting in my skin. I finally reached the phone, but minutes dragged by as I slumped against the wall trying to direct my brain in a straight enough line to remember Mama's phone number. Finally, I was able to dial.

"Hello?"

"Mama?" I immediately began to sob, hunched against the wall, clinging to the receiver like a drowning man to a life preserver. "You've just got to come and get me out of this place! *Please*. If you love me even one ounce right now, you'll come and get me. . . . *Please*, Mama."

She didn't tell me she couldn't come because she lived eleven hours away. Or that she'd try to make it tomorrow. Or that her car was broken down. She said, "*No.* I'm not going to come and get you, because you need to be exactly where you are."

It must have killed her to tell me that with me crying in her ear. By the time I gave up begging and laying on the guilt, she was crying too. But she wouldn't change her mind. Crushed, I hung up the phone, hobbled back to my room, and lay back down in a pool of my own sweat.

the prodigal comes home

Day Four: Dawn came, and with it, waves of nausea that blew up like a storm. A metallic taste rinsed through my mouth and set my jaws tingling as if I were biting aluminum. Simultaneously, my gut sent a red alert to my brain: *Get up now!*

I jumped out of bed and lunged toward the heavy institutional door leading into the bathroom. I rammed the handle, lunged through the door, and sprayed red projectile vomit on three walls and the tile-covered floor. Then I fell to my knees, grabbed the toilet rim, and vomited up what was left of Rita's red Gatorade. My legs quivered weakly underneath me, and dry heaves hit me, each blasting a new kind of pain through my limbs. The downward force of the heaves sent diarrhea rushing through my bowels. I couldn't get up onto the toilet fast enough, and that let loose, mingling with the red retch that already covered the floor.

Drowning in embarrassment, I crawled on my hands and knees, tears falling into the muck. A paper towel dispenser was bolted to the wall near the ceramic sink. I crawled there and stretched up and snatched a handful of towels. Turning back, I began to weep uncontrollably as I swiped the brown towels hopelessly through the mess, slopping it up and stuffing the towels in the toilet.

This was the lowest. I was alone, crawling through my own waste. My sobs echoed off the cold tile, and I tried to wipe my eyes with my forearms to keep the mess off my face. My misery was white-hot, unbearable. I hated life, I hated myself, I hated Norman, Lisa, Marabeth—every event that ever led me here.

At that moment, I begged God to rescue me or to let me die. Either one would have been fine.

+ chapter thirty-seven +

That was the day I realized I was trapped in detox for the duration, and I gave up trying to manipulate my way out. After cleaning up the bathroom and myself as best I could, I made my way back to the pay phone and called the Councils. It seemed so ironic that when Topper had first started praying for me years before—back when I thought I was completely in control of my life—I'd held the phone away from my ear and rolled my eyes at Missy. Now I deeply needed to hear the conviction in his voice, the prayers of a man who *knew* God heard him, who was certain that God still loved a sorry wreck like me.

Glorious got on the line first, always a person who lived by the Scripture "Weep with those who weep." I was so weak that when I started to speak, getting each word out was like lifting a heavy stone. I whispered into the phone, two or three words at a time, telling Glorious how desperate I was.

"I can't do this," I said. "I don't think I'm going to make it."

She cried with me and told me how sorry she was that I had to go through this much pain. Then she said, "Things are going to turn out fine, Michael. I promise you, God is going to get you through this."

Then Topper came on the line, and I asked him to pray for me. He had prayed for me every time we had spoken for more than five years. But this was the first time I had ever asked him to pray.

"God, Michael really needs you right now . . . ," was how he began.

Topper Council knew every awful thing I had done, but he had never

condemned me and had never turned away from me. Now I was like a sink-
ing ship in a storm, and he was a lighthouse, offering hope in the distance,
something to aim for, even if I didn't make it. When he finished his prayer,
I prayed aloud myself. It was the first time in years that I'd prayed when
someone else could hear me. Then Topper recited to me a part of Psalm 23,
ending with, "Yea, though I walk through the valley of the shadow of death,
I will fear no evil: for thou art with me."

"That's where you are right now, Michael," he said, "in the valley of the
shadow of death. But God is with you, so you don't need to be afraid."

That night in my room, I rummaged through my duffel bag and pulled
out my Bible. I hadn't opened it for years, but when I packed for detox, I had
put the leather-bound book in with my clothes, just in case. Now I opened it
and began to read. Verses jumped out at me full of new meaning, and I underlined them with a pen: "Come to me, all you who are weary and burdened,
and I will give you rest." "Jesus said to them, 'It is not the healthy who need a
doctor, but the sick. I have not come to call the righteous, but sinners.'"

As I turned through the Gospels, randomly it seemed, tears blurred my
vision, then dropped onto the pages like raindrops. Then I turned to the
Gospel of Luke and began to weep openly again: "I will set out and go back to
my father and say to him: Father, I have sinned against heaven and against you.
I am no longer worthy to be called your son; make me like one of your hired
men.' . . . The father said to his servants, 'Quick! Bring the best robe and put
it on him. Put a ring on his finger and sandals on his feet. Bring the fattened
calf and kill it. Let's have a feast and celebrate. For this son of mine was dead
and is alive again; he was lost and is found.' So they began to celebrate."

I knew that Topper and Glorious were right, that I was walking through
the valley of the shadow of death, but there was a way back. No matter how
far from God I had wandered, He would not turn me away if I came with a
humble and repentant heart. My mind ached. My soul cried out. And for the
first time in years, I listened with all my heart for the still, small voice of God.

+ chapter thirty-eight +

As detox wound down, so did I. At thirty-eight years old, I was a wreck of a man, completely drained. I would sit in the relaxation room staring off into space with my mouth hanging open until there was some reason to get up. Then, like a cripple, I'd brace myself on the chair arms and slowly hike myself up. While walking, I could barely put one foot in front of the other and had to hold myself up by leaning a hand on walls or furniture.

The withdrawal anxiety stayed with me, and my stomach felt as if I'd jumped from an airplane and was still falling. On day five, I started eating again. Lisa, Missy, and Megan came to see me and brought hot baked potato soup. Two more days, and I'd be going home. That's when I began hearing talk of another institution.

A Vanderbilt therapist suggested that I go to a twenty-eight-day rehab program. "I really feel like that's what you need to do," she said to me in my room.

"I don't care what you think I need to do," I snapped. "I'm *not* leaving here and going to another place for twenty-eight days!"

I felt that nine days of detox was plenty. I was clean, and I wanted to be around clean, positive people. But Lisa and Missy thought I should go too. I put up a fight, but in the end I listened to my lawyer. David thought if he could show a judge that I had successfully completed both programs, it would help my case. I can never know how things might have turned out had

the prodigal comes home

I not gone to rehab, but I do know this: in rehab I got cleaner and more determined both to stay clean and to help others — but through the friends I made there, I learned more about drugs, kinds of drugs, and how to get them, than I knew before I went in.

After all I'd done to her, Lisa still wanted to make sure I got well, so she picked me up and drove me to a place called Cumberland Heights. Night surrounded us as she steered her car up a road that led through wide fields and meadows to a complex of one-story wood-frame buildings, well lit and spread over five or six acres. Lisa helped me check in, and I found out I had to spend one night in Cumberland's detox center. That turned out to be like a spa vacation compared to the lockdown I'd just come from. Addicts could come and go, walk the grounds, even leave if they wanted to.

On that first night at Cumberland, I definitely wanted to leave. Lisa said good-bye and I wandered into a television room where a bunch of new guys were sitting around enthusiastically comparing their addictions. Most had arrived there directly from their collapsed lives, rather than through another institution like me, and were just beginning to deal with their problems. There was Rick, a rock-hard bodybuilder and hardcore cocaine addict. He was covered with bandages and scabs because, after putting some junk coke in his veins, he'd had a bad hallucination and jumped through a window. Another guy, Johnny, was also a cokehead and just about as hick-town, blue-collar as you could get: John Deere ball cap, lace-up boots, and a pinch of Copenhagen riding in his cheek. As Rick yakked cheerfully about his injuries, Johnny leaned forward, elbows on his knees, quietly spitting brown juice into a Styrofoam cup.

Then there was Miller. An alcoholic from New Orleans, he wore a yellow bomber jacket. He had straight, sandy brown hair parted down the middle and an enormous, shaggy mustache that hung like drapes around a mouth that contained about twelve rotting teeth. When Miller talked, he barely moved his lips, and you could hardly understand him. That was just as well, because he had a hard gaze that made it seem he'd just as soon kill you as look at you. Later I found out the police suspected him of murder.

As these men and others laughed over their horror stories, I sank way back in a chair, trying my best to disappear into the long, black jacket I was wearing. *Oh dear Lord, get me out of here,* was all I could think. I'd been around other addicts, but they had been *celebrity* addicts or at least people on the fringes of the music world. I have to admit, I thought I didn't belong here with salesmen and truck drivers and mill workers down on their luck. Looking back, though, I can tell you two things. First, I became good friends with several of those guys, which punched holes in my stuck-up attitude. Second, the collection of people in that room underlined this fact: addiction doesn't discriminate.

In rehab I met a number of people who were addicted to painkillers just like I was. And here's one of the scariest things I learned: the problem with painkiller addiction is that most people consider it a celebrity copout—an excuse the stars make for other kinds of bad behavior. In some cases, maybe it is, but painkiller addiction isn't just celebrity territory. It's a problem that affects Main Street as much as Hollywood Boulevard, Music Row, and Rodeo Drive. Why? As I said before, when you're depressed or under pressure, painkillers can make you forget your troubles. Second, painkiller addicts can function beautifully for years without anyone ever realizing they're addicts because they cruise through their days and are easygoing and fun to be around. At first. That's why I liked taking pills before I went clubbing. Third, painkillers are one of the few addictions that insurance will pay for. Housewives and executives and truck drivers addicted to painkillers don't have to hunt drugs in dark alleys like junkies sniffing for heroin.

At Cumberland, my days began at seven o'clock roll call and progressed through 12-step meetings ("Hi, I'm Michael, and I'm an addict") and seminars on relationships, communication, goal-setting, and on and on. I learned a lot about why I used the pills (both to escape and to belong) and what they did to my body (wrecked my liver), as well as strategies for staying clean.

Through all of it, though, the thing that struck me most was the utter hopelessness of a healing program that centered on a multiple-choice god. While working our way through the twelve steps, which include things like admitting that you're an addict and making amends to the people you've hurt, counselors told us to stake our recoveries on "a higher power of your own choosing."

"It doesn't matter what that person or thing is," they told us. It could be a doorknob or a tree, as long as we believed it could help us. That went against everything I had ever known. My God *made* the trees. I'm not an evangelist, but in that place I made sure everyone knew what I believed, that my higher power was Christ and that my God was the God of all gods, the God of the ages, or there would be no reason for me to be in that place, because there would be no hope.

+ chapter thirty-nine +

Sometimes some of us took a van ride for an "outside" meeting, for example, to a Narcotics Anonymous meeting at one church or another in Nashville. Sitting in a circle discussing my addiction seemed a long way down from my last night at the Grand Ole Opry. I can't count how many times I wished for my old life back. Those kinds of thoughts pierced me most during some of the group "trust exercises" we did on Wednesdays and Fridays. One was the classic "trust fall," except that in this case you stood up on a perch and fell six feet into the arms of your "group." But it was a different exercise that made me feel so ridiculous, so stupid, so childish, so far down at the bottom of life's barrel that I wanted to tear out my hair in frustration over having ruined my own life.

Our "facilitator"—I'll call him Brian—led about ten of us out to a wooded area near the river that flowed through the property. Brian had done us the favor of taking a long roll of twine and winding it around and through some trees in a crisscrossing path that was supposed to lead from a starting point to a finish line. One at a time, each of us had to put on a blindfold and work our way from the start to the end by feeling our way along the string. When each person took his turn, the rest of us stood far enough away so that we couldn't hear what Brian was saying to whoever was doing the exercise.

When my turn came, I walked over to the trees and stood next to him. In front of me, I could see the white twine zigging and zagging from one tree to the next, sometimes crossing back on itself before moving forward again to a point about twenty feet into the woods.

Brian smiled his counseling smile. "Ready?"

"Sure," I said. This was about day seven, and even though I had become determined to stay off drugs, I was already way over some of the touchy-feely parts of the program. Brian handed me a dark scarf. I slipped it down over my head and across my eyes. Then Brian took my hands and placed them on the string.

"Okay, Michael. Go."

Slowly, I moved forward. The sunlight beamed through the blindfold so that the insides of my eyelids appeared red. I could smell dirt and leaves and hear the call of jays from high in the trees. At first the course seemed straight-forward, and I moved ahead with no problem, feeling my way left, then right, making steady progress. Gradually, though, I slowed . . . then stopped. Had I made mistakes where the string crossed itself? Was I now moving back-ward? I fumbled forward again, the dry twine sliding through my hands. Minutes passed. Doubt crept in. I was no longer sure whether the string led forward or back in the direction I'd come from. I stopped again, disoriented.

Turning my head in a slow arc, I listened for clues but heard only jays and the shimmer of leaves. A few steps more. *No!* I was sure I was headed back toward Brian now. I imagined the rest of the group, probably having a good laugh watching me grope around like an idiot. Spinning on my shoe in the dirt, I took several confident steps in the other direction. But then the twine angled sharply off to the left, and I stopped again, blind and confused.

Then a thought hit me like a punch in the gut. *I am a thirty-eight-year-old disgraced, divorced, ruined fool playing mind games in the woods with strangers.* Suddenly defeat dropped over me like a lead blanket.

I stood still and let go of the string. "I can't do it."

"What?" Brian said. I could hear him striding toward me, his shoes crunching leaves.

"I can't find the end." I started to take the blindfold off, but he stopped me.

"No, no," he said. "What do you need?"

"What?"

"What do you *need?*"

"I need to get to the end of the string."

"Yes, but what do you *need?*" Brian repeated.

My faced flushed. I felt my temper rising. "What do you mean, what do I *need?*"

"Michael, what do you *need* to get to the end?"

"I *need* someone to tell me where it is!" I said, mocking him. "I *need* help!"

"That's *right!*" Brian said cheerfully. "You got it! You can take the blind-fold off now."

That was it? That's what this was about? I wanted to hit him in the mouth. The whole point of the exercise, it turned out, was that it couldn't be done. It was set up to be impossible to get from the start to the finish. As soon as you asked for help, you "passed."

I glared at Brian and stormed out of the woods. Suddenly I was furious with David, with everyone for saying this would help me. At that moment, I felt it was all for show, so that I would look good in front of the judge. I was selling the song again, performing like a trained monkey, mouthing the right words, doing what everyone else said to do. And what angered me more than anything else about it was that I *had* to keep selling it whether I liked it or not, had to keep going through the motions, because the only thing I had left to lose was my freedom.

+ chapter forty +

Mama and Aunt Linda came to see me in rehab. Mike Curb and his wife did too. They let me know they were behind me and that we would work through this. I began to feel that even though I had clearly broken the law and definitely made a long series of stupid and selfish choices, addiction wasn't the same kind of moral failure as the affair with Marabeth. Instead, I was sick. And I was getting help.

It was in that spirit that a group of us from rehab—Rick, Johnny, Miller, and Steve, another guy I'd met—kept in touch after we left Cumberland. We got together as kind of a loose support group, sometimes meeting at a hotel and ordering food, sometimes gathering at my apartment. But one by one, my rehab friends dropped like flies back into their old worlds. I tried to stay strong, but almost immediately after I left Cumberland, there was an early sign that I might head down the wrong path.

I had to launch *Heaven to Earth* on TBN in a concert that had been scheduled long before I got busted. But I had sold a lot of my stage clothes to get drugs, and finding something appropriate to wear wasn't easy. In the old days, I would've gone out and dropped $1,000 on an outfit. But I was broke, and through detox and rehab, I'd also lost about twenty-five pounds. I didn't have many clothes that still fit, but I was kind of excited about trying on some things I hadn't worn in a while.

One day at my apartment, Missy was in the kitchen fixing something to eat while I dug deep into my bedroom closet. I pulled out a black sport jacket I hadn't worn since my clubbing days, when I had been in a lot better shape, and was surprised and happy when it fit. Standing in front of the mirrored closet door, I kind of modeled it for myself. Then I slipped my hands into the pockets, and fear sucked my breath away.

My fingertips touched pills.

It couldn't have been worse if I had put my hand into a pocketful of scorpions. With the same magnetic dread that pulled me to look under Mama's vanity cabinet, I brought the pills out to look at them. I didn't need to, though. I could have been blind and told you that it was three Oxys and three Norcos—the best of the best—just by the way they felt. My hands began to shake. I pulled off the jacket, laid it on the bed, stepped back, and crossed my arms. What was I going to do?

If you've never been an addict, that might seem like a lot of drama. *What's the big deal? Flush the pills down the toilet and get on with your life.* I wish it had been that simple. But for me, finding them was like accidentally running into someone from one of those toxic yet magnetic relationships, that person you never want to see again but can't live without. I was like a freshly dry drunk with an open bar tab or a recovering kleptomaniac left alone with diamonds.

Missy was in the other room. I could've told her what I'd found. Instead, I wrapped the pills in tissue and put them in a drawer.

ON TBN, I FELT BETTER and sang better than I had in years. I loved the new material and felt *Heaven to Earth* was one of my strongest records yet.

I also tried to be very honest on the program and shared a little about what I'd been through with drugs. Jan Crouch liked what she saw and offered to let me keep doing *The Michael English Show.* It seemed a good fit for me because it meant I could cut back on traveling and concentrate on my recovery.

But instead of working on recovery, I mainly worked on how to dabble in drugs without getting hooked. I had continued to see my Cumberland friends, even after they began slipping back into their old habits. About two months after rehab, Rick, the bodybuilder, came over to my apartment. He'd just had surgery on his hand to repair some of the damage he'd done when he jumped out the window. He'd always worn a fanny pack at rehab—once he'd unzipped it to show us the cocaine residue inside—and the day he came over, it was full of pills. Vicodin.

"You know what, dude?" Rick said. "As long as you don't keep doing it, you can take one of these and just see how it feels to you now. It won't hurt you. If you want one, take it."

For the life of me, I can't remember when I took that first pill, but it wasn't right away. I remember the battle that raged in my mind, like the old cartoons where an angel sits on one shoulder and a demon on the other.

"Think of everything you've been through," the angel said. "You don't want to have to go through that again."

"It's going to be awhile before your court date," the demon came back. "A few pills won't show up in a urine test by then."

"But you don't know how much your body can tolerate now," the angel protested. "If you take as many as before, you could be dead."

"Oh, come *on*, Mike, it takes awhile to get addicted," said the demon. "Just a couple won't hurt."

I wrestled back and forth like that until finally I threw my head back and chucked some pills down my throat.

+ chapter forty-one +

Still trying to get back in the swing of things, I got on a bus with my band and traveled all night to Idaho to play a state fair. We were continuing to promote *Heaven to Earth*, and I was still unsure of how the public would receive me. I had gone through detox and rehab, but so had other singers. But the unlawful stuff—the police, the news stories, the pending trial—that might be a different ball game in the public's eye.

I so appreciated Mike Curb sending me out, still putting me on the road. He easily could have said, "We're done with you. You're not a good investment," and washed his hands of me. Instead, he stood in there with me through some very tough times.

In Idaho we set up on a big stage in the middle of a racetrack. It was a casual outdoor event with "concert seating," people standing right down in front of the stage. Farther back, people were grouped on picnic blankets and lawn chairs, with bleacher seating behind them. We took the stage, and I had just launched into my first song when I looked down and saw Marcie Stambaugh standing right down front. Her blond hair was cut short, and she was wearing a sleeveless red turtleneck sweater and jeans. She and her friend Melissa were laughing and talking. Suddenly, as though she could feel my eyes on her, she looked up at me and smiled.

She was just as pretty as she had been in Michigan, with a brilliant, friendly smile and eyes shaped like almonds and turned up at the corners. I was single, and I admit it, I started to flirt. She flirted back, being silly, yelling out requests for me to sing certain songs.

"I forgot the words to that one," I'd say, grinning.

"I'll tell them to you," she'd called back.

After the concert, I saw Marcie and Melissa in the autograph area. I asked my road manager to invite Marcie and Melissa to dinner. They said yes.

Later that evening, she and Melissa brought some takeout food—Denny's or something—to my room at the hotel where we were staying. That might sound inappropriate, but it really was innocent. The two of them, a couple of guys from the band, and I just sat around talking and eating. They were on vacation, it turned out, and they decided to come see my concert. I remember watching Marcie in her red sweater. She kicked off her shoes and plopped down on the bed, lying on her side, elbow bent, her head propped on her hand, just talking away. I thought, *Well, this young lady's just going to be herself no matter what.* She was outgoing—fresh and fun. I found myself very attracted to her, but I knew I wasn't ready to jump into another relationship.

I didn't know it at the time, but the feeling she had of being drawn to me renewed itself that night. I never would have known it. She wasn't silly or girly or overly flirtatious. I didn't find out until more than a year later, but when she and Melissa left that night, Marcie left me a message at the front desk that included her phone number. She was desperate to be rid of what she considered a ridiculous feeling. "If he calls me," she told God, "it was meant to be. If not, it's just a silly little crush, me being crazy."

I never got the message. Marcie moved on with her life and began dating a guy named Rob. And when he asked her to marry him, she said yes.

+ chapter forty-two +

That first Vicodin that Rick gave me led me back to the bedroom drawer where I'd stashed the Oxys and Norcos from my jacket pocket. Then I began to party with the Cumberland guys, getting more pills. Steve had a connection. I was careful; I took just a few pills here and there, then purposely went for three days without. This way, I reasoned with myself, I could get a little buzz on without getting addicted again. Also, I'd learned in rehab that narcotics disappear from your system in just a few days. I had to go in and see David Raybin and, at least once, the arresting officers in my case. I was never sure when I'd have to take a urine test.

At first it seemed to be working. I'd go the three days, no problem. Then those days passed more slowly as I looked forward to being able to get high again. Then I began to count the days like a prisoner scratching tally marks on a jail cell wall. As my trial neared, I took more and more pills. Steve kept me supplied, scoring pills from a big guy he knew whose name was also Steve. So now I had two suppliers, a Big Steve and a Little Steve. Then Rick started bringing cocaine to my house and shooting up in the back bedroom. Once, when we were all sitting around partying, he spread a few lines of coke on the table.

"Let me try a hit of that," I said.

And I did. I took a rolled-up dollar bill and snorted it. Later I tried heroin. Never in my life would I have considered putting a needle in my vein. *That's crazy!* I used to think. *Only the lowest, most pathetic gutter junkies do that.* And yet I did it—only a couple of times, but that's not the point. Once is enough to kill you.

This is the pattern of addiction: a gradual breakdown of boundaries so that you wind up doing things you never would have dreamed of doing and hanging around people you never would have dreamed of hanging around with. It's self-destruction by degrees, a domino effect of one stupid decision after another, each one not a huge risk in itself but, when combined, a blueprint for disaster. The wickedest part is that after rehab, I *knew* I was headed for disaster. I hated it but was powerless to stop it, like a man lost at sea who becomes so exhausted he finally gives himself up to drown.

Soon I was in total free fall. I'd gone from sold-out and sober, gung ho, even wanting to become a drug counselor, straight back to addiction—only this time surrounded by a cast of junkies and felons. It was the *feeling* the pills gave me. Just as before, when I was on them, I could forget about the toilet my life had become. And that feeling was enough to seduce me to risk my freedom, to deceive me into believing it was worth it.

AFTER A SERIES OF DELAYS, my court date came. On June 16, 2000, I met David at the courthouse. He warned me that the press would be there. Apparently they monitored the court's docket. I didn't consider my case important, but the Nashville media always enjoyed a celebrity case. The fact that I was a Christian singer added a nice touch of irony to my story—hypocrisy makes wonderful headlines. I deeply resented that but also understood it and was ashamed.

"Now listen," David told me. "We're going to walk in and take an elevator up to the courtroom. As soon as the elevator opens, that's where the media will hit you. I want you to smile and act like everything's going to be fine. I'll do the talking."

I was used to reporters, of course. I had done plenty of interviews for television, radio, and magazines. After concerts I'd sometimes talk to the press. When you're at the top of your game, sparkling flashbulbs and microphones are part of the business. They help publicize your work. At the courthouse that night, though, they were completely different. The instant the elevator doors slid open, a row of television cameras surged toward me. Mainly, I remember impressions: Flashes popping. The NBC peacock logo, the CBS eye. Microphones being jabbed in my face. Reporters jostling each other, calling out questions.

I just shook my head and kept a humble "I'd love to talk, but I can't" look on my face. What I wanted to do was cover my ears and run.

David, meanwhile, held up his hands and smiled graciously: "Ladies and gentlemen, we can't talk to you right now, but as soon as this is over, we'll have a statement for you." He loves that kind of stuff, and he's good at it.

Inside the courtroom, I sat with David at the defendant's table. I had been charged with twelve counts of prescription fraud and was facing up to twelve years in prison. But David had told me with confidence that if I did what he said, I'd get off with a lighter sentence. With the judge looking down on me, scanning papers, holding my future in his hands, I felt like a complete loser. I felt dirty, ugly, wrong. I was embarrassed and even more deeply ashamed because I knew I hadn't done what David had asked me in good faith to do: stay off drugs.

With guilt and shame racing through my veins like fire, I waited through the formalities of the trial. I flashed back to Marabeth's pregnancy test. Once again I was waiting to find out how my life was going to turn out. In the end, the judge sentenced me to three years' probation, two hundred hours of community service, and a fine.

+ chapter forty-three +

One weekend in September, I went to visit Jackie McCall and her family in Cincinnati. That Sunday God showed me the enormous, lasting cost of public sin and the two faces of His church, like opposite sides of the same coin.

Since meeting Jackie, I had grown especially close to her father, Lloyd, a jolly, big-bellied man who would have made a perfect Santa Claus. Saturday evening over dinner, Jackie, Lloyd, and Verna, Jackie's mother, started talking about their church, and someone pitched out the idea of me going to church with them the next day. But for me, church was mostly a thing of the past. Every so often I might end up visiting some random congregation on a Sunday morning, but I didn't have a home church. Not only was I not close to God in my heart, but I worried about people giving me "the look"—a knowing glance of the kind the people at North East Free Will Pentecostal may have given a hooker.

But Lloyd and Verna were good people. They were always throwing out hints and ideas, trying to get me to come back to church. They never pressured me.

So that evening when Lloyd said, "You ought to come to church with us tomorrow, maybe even sing a song," for some reason, I said I would.

Lloyd heaved himself up from the dining table, grinning. "We'll get this worked out right now!" he said and snatched up the telephone to call one of the assistant pastors.

the prodigal comes home

"He said to just come on up in the morning," Lloyd reported back to us. "Said he'd see what he could work out."

You may have noticed I haven't named the church or the minister. There's a reason for that. The next day Lloyd drove us there in his pickup truck, arriving a little early at the white clapboard building that looked like someone had converted a good-sized one-story home into a church and built onto it. The sanctuary was small and plain, with eight or nine rows of pews arched in three columns around a low stage. Only a handful of worshipers were there ahead of us. I don't remember exactly why, but I remember that the sanctuary seemed dim, as though heavy drapes blocked sunlight from the room. The only lights were shining on people up near the pulpit, where half a dozen people were rehearsing praise songs before the service.

I took a seat in the back pew. That had become my habit. I told myself it was because I was six-four and didn't want to block anyone's view. But in my other life, I had sat in the front row at church on many Sundays, never worrying about my height. The truth was, since my public fall, I didn't want anyone to notice I was there. My low-profile policy didn't work that day, though. Lloyd, Jackie, and the others had remained in the foyer, huddled up with some official-looking folks from the church. I noticed that the conversation went on for a long time. Meanwhile, a few people had begun to trickle into the sanctuary. Suddenly Jackie walked up behind me and tapped my shoulder.

"Come here," she said, moving back the way we'd come in.

Confused, I got up and followed her out to the foyer. I thought she wanted me to talk with someone about singing arrangements. Instead, she led me past Lloyd and Verna, all the way out the front door into the parking lot.

"I'm so mad! I'm so ticked off!" Jackie fumed, walking quickly toward her father's truck.

"What's going on?"

"Just get in the truck, and I'll tell you."

We climbed in and shut the doors. "Not only do they not want you to sing," Jackie began, "but they think your presence here will be distracting and take away from the service."

"You've *got* to be kidding me."

Too worn out from living to be angry, I laughed. Two or three years earlier, this would have been the last straw for me. I would have raged about the hypocrisy of Christians and sworn on my grandma's grave never to cross a church threshold again. But my heart was starting to change. I thought of Jim Cymbala and Brooklyn Tab. I thought of the Gaithers and the Councils. Christianity was a messy club, but it did have wonderful members. It seemed my bitterness had begun to unravel at the edges. Jackie was still embarrassed and griping out loud, and I didn't blame her. But I just shook my head and sighed: *Man. It's pretty bad when you get kicked out of church.*

By then Lloyd, Verna, and the others had joined us. Then I blurted something out that surprised even me: "How far is Solid Rock Church from here?"

"Not far," Jackie said.

"Let's go there," I said.

Solid Rock is a huge church in Monroe, Ohio, whose massive modern building pokes up so that you can see it from the interstate. When we drove up, the parking lot was packed. Inside, the sanctuary was bright, with colorful banners hanging from the ceiling, rows and rows of pews fanning out in a semicircle from the stage, and a big rear balcony overlooking the main floor. Church had already started. An usher found us seats four or five rows from the back. I tried to make myself as small as possible, not wanting to be noticed. At the other church, I had rolled with the punches, but that didn't mean I was ready for another round.

Only a few minutes passed before I felt another tap on my shoulder.

"Mr. English, could I see you for a minute?" A name-tagged usher stood behind me and motioned me toward the back of the sanctuary.

My stomach dropped. *No, this can't happen twice in one day—or twice in one lifetime.*

I wanted to say, "I promise I'll put my head down and be good and not say a word. Just let me stay here. Please." Instead, I got up and followed the usher out.

"The pastor would like to see you," he said after we'd stepped out of the sanctuary. Then he led me through another door.

the prodigal comes home

Have you ever been called to the principal's office? That sort of sick dread you get in your stomach was exactly the feeling I had as I followed the usher through a hallway that circled the right rear of the sanctuary. As we passed one, two, three doors on the left, I nearly held my breath, wondering what my punishment would be this time. I could hear the muted singing from inside the church, and the voices grew louder as we went. When we reached the fourth door, the usher pushed it open, and the full-throated sound of a choir hit me like splashes of spring water, cool and refreshing.

Through the door, I could see the pulpit area, the pastor seated with his wife and a few other ministers, and the choir in front of them. There were a lot of black voices in the mix, and all of the singers were just ripping it up. There's something about the open tones of black men singing that lifts my soul. There's not a better sound. In my imagination, I picture angels being able to sing any way they want to; I'm sure that's the way they would want to sing.

The pastor, Lawrence Bishop, was a good-looking, silver-haired man. His wife, Darlene, also preached at the church. He looked up and saw me, then motioned for me to come and sit beside him. When I did, he reached over and put his hand on my knee. "I'm glad you're here, Michael," he said.

My throat closed, and I wanted to cry. But I was glad I didn't, because right then Pastor Lawrence leaned over again and asked me to sing.

I whispered back, "I don't have any tracks with me."

"That's okay," he said. "They'll follow you."

After a little church business, the announcements, and so forth, Pastor Lawrence got up and introduced me. "We have a special guest for you this morning. Michael English came to church here this morning, and we're going to have him sing a song."

The congregation broke into applause.

I stood and walked to the microphone. I was so tired of being angry. I wanted something eternal, something that I once knew, something that was so good before it got all clouded and foul. I wanted to reach up somehow or other and grab hold of God instead of trusting in man. I knew He was doing good things in my heart by then. I knew that, because I was getting ready to sing in church just after a blow that easily could have landed me in a bar, drinking and pilling on a Sunday morning. And I wanted the people at Solid Rock to know how much their acceptance meant to me.

"Before I sing, I just want you guys to know what my morning was like," I said. "I just came from a church that basically asked me to leave. I'm not telling this story to make you feel sorry for me. I'm telling it to let you know that this is what I would have missed out on if I had gotten angry and put my tail between my legs and gone home, which is what I'd have done most of my life.

"I guess the moral of the story is never to give up," I went on. "No matter how bad things seem—and to me, that would be just about the worst, to come to a church and have them say, 'You're not welcome here'—never give up."

Then I sang "His Eye Is on the Sparrow," and I'll never forget it as long as I live. I began a cappella:

Why should I feel discouraged . . .

The crowd went crazy, clapping and shouting amens. I continued:

Why should the shadows come,
Why must my heart feel lonely
And long for heaven and home,
When Jesus is my portion?
My constant friend is He:
His eye is on the sparrow,
And I know He watches me.

The band joined me in key, and I started singing the chorus.

I sing because I'm happy,
I sing because I'm free,
His eye is on the sparrow,
And I know he watches me

the prodigal comes home

The lyrics were so perfect for that morning that I began to weep:

I know He loves me . . .
I know He forgives me . . .

The congregation stood and began praising God, weeping with me. It seemed the Holy Spirit had fallen on the sanctuary in a special way. I finished the song and felt an unbelievable sense of welcome and compassion. I could hardly believe that a morning so dark with rejection could turn out this way. That day taught me a lesson that would repeat itself: when the lowest thing that could possibly happen happens, don't give up, because you might be missing a blessing just down the road.

+ chapter forty-four +

Topper Council had always encouraged me with words about God's love and patience, but he'd always been straight with me too.

"God only gives us so many chances," Topper would say. "He's a God of mercy, but He'll let you go your own way if you keep on."

As much as I resented the people at Jackie's church for asking me to leave, maybe it was a hint or a warning from God that He knew I was fully involved in drugs again even if it wasn't immediately obvious to others.

For six months I moved out to California to do *The Michael English Show* at TBN's studios in Tustin, about thirty minutes south of LA. It would have been paradise, except that all I could think of was how to get more pills. Norman says now that when he watches tapes of those California shows, he can tell I was high. But I hid it well. The Crouches did cancel the show, but it was over a misunderstanding between me and one of their pastor-guests.

I moved back to Nashville and for a while was basically homeless. I had run out of money and was six months behind in my car payments. The repo man came looking for me, but Mama and Daddy chipped in $500 apiece and bailed me out. In seven years, I had gone from being at the top of my profession, living in an enormous house, and having a string of zeros in my bank account, to being broke with no place to live. Worse, I was a junkie again.

Then things really started to go downhill.

For four months in 2001, I lived with a friend named Seth in a ranch-style house off Granny White Pike that was split into apartments. An incident that happened that September shows how dangerous I had become to myself and others—and that I would have been dead long ago if it wasn't for my friends.

I know this story only because Missy and Seth were there and told me what I did. I barely remember any of it. I had run out of pills, but I did have money—I don't know how; maybe I had gotten a royalty check—and a hookup. All I had to do was get myself to London, Kentucky. I had called a connection there who told me he could get me Oxys. The problem was that I was in no shape to drive. When Missy came over that evening, I was already going into withdrawals, frantic, pacing the floor and muttering, "I'm out, I'm out. I've gotta get some pills. I don't know what I'm going to do."

I clenched and unclenched my fist, and as I wore a rut in the carpet, my thighs quivered as if I might collapse any second. "I need to get to Kentucky," I told Missy.

"I can't take you, Michael."

"I know you can't, I know you can't," I mumbled half to myself. I ran my hands through my hair, still moving, always moving.

I looked at Seth, and he shook his head. "I'm not taking you, man."

I didn't tell them, but I had taken four Ambien sleeping pills. I had to take something. I couldn't deal with the withdrawals cold, with nothing to take the edge off. When my jitters started fading into a weird giddiness, Missy hid the keys to my car. Then she and Seth went into the kitchen to fix something to eat. I must have known her hiding places, because Missy says that the next thing she and Seth heard was an enormous crash out in front of the house.

Missy and Seth ran outside and found me standing beside my black Lexus LS 400 shaking my head. "I can't believe I did this. . . . I gotta get to Kentucky. . . . I can't believe I did this."

I had backed the Lexus partway down the long driveway but must have fishtailed and lost control. The front end of the car was perpendicular to the driveway, and the back end was suspended over a three-foot ditch, the bumper wedged solidly into the far embankment.

"I can't believe I did this," I repeated.

"Thank God you did this!" Missy snapped. "If you would've made it out of this driveway, you'd have killed yourself and probably someone else."

"You're right, you're right," I said. "I need to go back in the house."

Missy says we all hiked back up the driveway, leaving the car where I'd crashed it, since there was no way to get it out. I didn't give the crash a second thought. All I cared about was finding another way to get the Oxys.

"You've got to find someone to go get them for me," I told Missy. She called my friend Tony Tolliver and told him how bad off I was. He agreed to go to Kentucky for me, said he'd leave right then and come over to get my money. By that time the Ambien had really kicked in. I was dazed and confused, talking nonsense.

"Michael, what did you take?" Missy demanded.

She says I snickered like a little kid with a secret. "I took four Ambien."

"Where are they?"

"I'm not telling," I said, giggling.

"Just give them to me," she said. "Just let me hold them for you."

Reluctantly, I handed her a bottle with a few pills left in it. When I wasn't looking, she hid the bottle under the fake moss at the base of one of my silk ficus trees.

Tony showed up, and I handed over the money, a thousand dollars cash. But after he left, I said to Missy, "I don't think he's going to do that for me. I need to take some more Ambien."

Missy wouldn't hand over the pills. "Michael, you just need to settle down and go to sleep."

But I wasn't ready to go to sleep. Instead, I started chasing Missy around the house. "I'm gonna getcha!" I said, giggling like a lunatic. "I'm gonna get those pills! You better give 'em to me!"

She says I sounded playful and goofy. She wanted to laugh, but she couldn't, because she knew that underneath my drug-induced silliness, I really was desperate for her to hand over the pills, and she needed to stay firm. Finally, I gave up. Hours later, with no pills or car keys to worry about, Missy fell asleep on the couch. But at around two thirty in the morning, she says, she woke up to find me smearing Jiff creamy peanut butter all over the television screen with my bare hands.

the prodigal comes home

"Oooooh, look at the *peanut* butter," I said, singsonging like I was admiring kittens.

Missy took the peanut butter away and finally got me to go to sleep, she says. As it turned out, I was right about Tony Tolliver. I spent the whole next day cussing him out because, after Seth pried my car out of the ditch, I was sober enough to get in it and drive to Kentucky. But Tony held on to my money so that I couldn't.

THAT WASN'T AS BAD as it got. Soon after I put my car in the ditch, Missy helped me find another apartment in Cool Springs. That's when things started to get really, really bad again. I never went out. I didn't bathe. The dog mess began to pile up again. I slept on the couch all day until Missy got off work and came over. She would clean up after the dogs and clean up the kitchen. Then I took some pills at five or six o'clock, and that perked me up for a while. I'd get a little jolly and want to watch TV and hang out and talk. But by ten o'clock I would doze off sitting up, then literally fall over sideways into a dead sleep.

I put Missy in a terrible position. At that point in my life, I had no one else. I had ruined every relationship I had. She couldn't keep me completely off the pills, because I had become so physically dependent again that sudden withdrawal could have sent me into respiratory failure, which she knew because she'd researched it. She didn't want to see me dead.

When she'd try to help me cut down by holding my pills, I became a raging, manipulative addict. I knew Missy loved me like a brother, and I knew how to make her angry the way a brother does, and how to draw her back.

Some people might say she enabled me, and in some ways maybe that's true. But I also know that if it hadn't been for Missy, I'd be dead. Many times, when I'd take too many pills, she would sit up at night and keep watch. That's because sometimes I stopped breathing.

+ chapter forty-five +

While I was at the Vanderbilt detox facility, the staff put an addict in my room who had a seizure so violent that he banged his head against the wall until blood ran down his face. That man told me how to get high faster on Oxycontin. By the fall of 2001, I was taking four or five Oxy 80s at once— enough to kill most people. Life swam by in a haze of sleep, pills, and beer. Big Steve was in and out of the apartment dealing drugs and keeping me supplied. I no longer went outside. I was heavy but not just overweight. I was *swollen*. My face was puffy and my skin as unhealthy and pale as a corpse. My feet and ankles were so thick I sometimes couldn't put on shoes. I wasn't booking any gigs because I had become an absolute slurring mess onstage. One of the last times I'd sung was near home in North Carolina. In the middle of the concert, I started wandering around onstage babbling nonsense, something about looking for my dogs—where were they and why couldn't I find them? The audience sat there with their mouths hanging open, stunned into silence by my rambling, boozy rant.

Curb Records was still my label, but I didn't have any new projects planned, and they weren't asking for any. I didn't care. I hated myself—what I had become. But I had also stopped trying to change. I can't tell you how many times I stood over the toilet holding all the pills I had left, thinking, *Okay, God, I'm going to do this. I'm going to flush these and You're going to sustain me. You're going to rescue me.*

But each time, I chickened out. The truth was, I was afraid God wouldn't rescue me, and I was terrified of what that would do to my little sliver of faith. And so I lost all hope. I gave up. All I cared about was getting enough pills in me to stave off the withdrawal horrors that would swoop down on me like demons if I didn't feed the addiction. But one night, in less than a minute, all that changed.

It was a normal evening: a handful of pills, a few beers, the television droning for hours as I floated along on my narcotic wave. I was home alone, lying on the couch with my back propped up in the corner. I can't tell you what happened or how, but suddenly my mind began to rise above my body. The next thing I knew, I was looking down on myself.

I have heard of people in Eastern religions having out-of-body experiences. I have heard of people seeing themselves in dreams. And I have heard people tell of dying on operating tables, rising above their own bodies, and looking down as surgeons worked to revive them. I don't know what happened to me that night in late 2001, but I do know that whatever it was, it was God-driven.

Looking down, I could see myself, and it was an unfamiliar image: *Who is this swollen, dirty, pathetic man?* But my mind's eye knew it was me. And for a moment in time, my thoughts were as clear as they are now. Then, as plain as audible speech, a still, small voice burned two simple questions into my conscience: *Is this the way you want it to end? Is this the way you want your daughter to remember you?*

I didn't *hear* the voice. But I was certain it was God, pressing the way He does, pressing on my heart, pressing me to realize that I had a choice: I could keep heading down the road of addiction and be dead at forty. Or I could follow Him back home and live to tell about it. It was a divine ultimatum, a black-and-white choice. And suddenly, in that rare, crystal-clear moment, I was struck by the knowledge that if I didn't change, God might remove His hand from me entirely and let me go my own way. My daughter might find me one day, lying dead on the couch, no different than any overdosed junkie in an alley.

Then just as suddenly, I was back in my body again, seeing through my normal eyes, and a torrent of emotions surged through me: anguish, the sense of an ultimate crossroads, but most of all, a holy fear.

I rolled off the couch, and my knees hit the floor. Hunched over the cushions, I buried my face in my hands. "I don't even feel worthy to be calling on Your name at this point, Lord," I whispered. "But if You'll help me get off these pills, if You'll help me get clean and do right, I'll do everything in my power to tell the world, and I won't be ashamed to tell it."

It wasn't a bargain I was making. It was a vow.

Shaken, I heaved myself back up on the couch and peered around the room as if someone might have seen me. *What* was *that? What just happened to me?* Whatever it was, I knew it wasn't my imagination, because conviction burned in my heart: I *had* to make a change, and I had to make it *now*.

I called Missy on the phone. "I've got to do something," I told her. "I've got to get off this stuff."

I didn't tell her about the out-of-body thing. In fact, I didn't tell anyone about it for a long time because I was pretty sure they'd think I was either hallucinating or crazy.

Missy and I discussed options. The next day we called Topper and Glorious in Paducah, and over the next week, we all traded ideas. I was certain of one thing: I didn't think I'd survive another trip to Vanderbilt. Then I heard about something called rapid opiate detoxification. The process compresses the entire withdrawal experience from nine or ten days to a matter of hours using Naltrexone, a drug that blocks the effects of opiates like heroin and Oxycontin. A medical team administers anesthesia and other drugs that speed up withdrawal so that the whole thing is over within four to six hours.

That sounded great to me. Missy researched some programs and found one in California. But the price was steep: $10,000. I didn't have that kind of money. Desperate, I called Mike Curb. Incredibly, he agreed to give me an advance on my next record—which at the time was about the same as just giving me the money, since he had every reason to believe I'd never deliver on my end of the deal.

It took some time to schedule my rapid detox appointment and make travel arrangements, but a couple of weeks later, Missy and her parents flew with me to California. A day and a half later, after lying in a hospital bed with the Naltrexone streaming through my veins and a morphine drip to ward off the pain, I was clean!

the prodigal comes home

I wanted to rejoice, I really did. But the process left me as wiped out as I had been after Vanderbilt. When we headed back to Nashville, the Councils had to wheelchair me through the airport like an old man.

As it turned out, it was too soon to celebrate. I had taken the trouble to get the drugs out of my system, but I had not thought to get the drug dealer out of my house. At first Big Steve seemed happy I had gotten off pills, and maybe he was. But once again I found that narcotic addiction is more than physical—it's a state of mind, a habit, a routine—like getting out of bed on one side or the other, or putting on your right shoe before your left. The patterns were deeply etched in me, especially the excuses. After four days, I was still wrung out, exhausted, barely able to take a step. And I knew that just one of Big Steve's pills would take away the awful, hateful weakness. It was too much.

My relapse lasted only two weeks before the conviction that had consumed me that night on the couch burned too badly for me to ignore it. I had made a promise to God. *I cannot keep taking these pills,* I thought. *I cannot make God a promise, then just spit in His face.*

I couldn't go to Missy again or to her parents. I couldn't go to Mike Curb. I had cashed in those chips already. But I had to do something. I was still on probation and tired of living a dirty, stinking, sinful life, hiding and scheming in order to slowly kill myself. Ironically, the person who gave me the answer was Little Steve.

He had mentioned something called the methadone program before. But I had dismissed it as a weakling's way to get off drugs, a way that junkies used to tide themselves over when they ran out of dope. But now I was desperate. I asked him if he could come over to my apartment and talk.

"Do you think you could help me get in there?" I asked him, referring to a methadone clinic in Nashville.

"I'll take you," he said. "I'll even call and get it set up."

I didn't know it then, but that was the first day of my second chance at life.

+ chapter forty-six +

When Little Steve talked to me about methadone before, I dismissed it, thinking it was just substituting one drug for another. That's not at all true. Of course, methadone is a drug, but not in the sense that it's something that you can take to get high. It's actually a medication that occupies the part of the brain that triggers withdrawal symptoms in people who are addicted to opiates like heroin and Oxycontin. To put it another way, methadone is a medication that tricks the brain into thinking it's getting opiates when it's not—and without delivering any sort of "high," euphoria, or mood change.

Of course, people have found ways to abuse methadone by combining it with other drugs. Isn't that often the nature of sin—that we take something good and twist it for evil? And that has given people a wrong impression of what methadone is. And that's sad, because people like me could get off drugs a lot sooner if they knew that by switching patients from an opiate to methadone, then slowly decreasing the dosage, doctors have successfully gotten addicts off heroin and other drugs for thirty years.

Walking into the clinic that day, I didn't know that. After my previous failures, I didn't even expect it to work. But all that changed within a week.

The program was a step-down plan. During the first level, I went to the clinic every day and received one oral dose of liquid methadone. Immediately, this accomplished two things: first, taking just one dose a day began to change my longtime habit of taking pills as many times a day as I could get them;

second, I had placed myself under a doctor's care. My probation officer knew about and approved the program. I didn't have to do anything illegal not to hurt anymore. Not only was I tired of hurting; I was also sick to death of having to do wrong just to keep from hurting. With the methadone, I didn't have to hide and sneak around. I didn't have to worry about where I was going to get another batch of pills every three days or how I was going to scrounge up the money to pay for them.

It was like waking up in a whole new world. Within a week, my days and nights normalized. I started doing basic things again—like bathing and eating. I began to enjoy breakfast in the morning, lunch at midday, and dinner in the evening. Who ever would have thought that the act of eating normal meals at normal times could seem so miraculous? But for years I had planned my eating around my pill taking in order to create the maximum buzz. Now I could eat when I was supposed to eat and actually taste food again and enjoy it. Meanwhile, the puffiness and swelling in my body started to dissipate. It didn't happen overnight, but I do remember the morning I woke up and saw my ankles for the first time in a long while. I nearly laughed aloud and said, "Hey! Where y'all been?"

After I proved I was committed to getting off pills, I started the next level of the program: "take-homes." That meant the doctor rationed out three days' worth of methadone and allowed me to take it on my own at home. Shortly after that, I began to work again, and a friend of mine, Renee Barham, starting booking me to sing in churches and other small venues.

After a few months at that level, the clinic supplied me with a month's worth of methadone. Then, slowly, the doctor began decreasing my doses. Sometimes days would go by and I would forget to take the medication. I just wasn't thinking about drugs anymore.

This was my miracle—to be so radically off course for so many years and then suddenly be back on the right road again with my compass pointed toward God. When I started driving my own life, as though God were like some kind of global positioning system that I could choose to follow or ignore, I turned down dead ends and dark alleys, thinking they were going to lead me somewhere. I thought I had gotten so good at choosing my own path that I didn't need God anymore. I had gotten, as the GPS in my car sometimes tells me, "off my specified route." But I finally got to a place where I knew I needed help. I was so lost I couldn't find my way home.

At my concerts, I've talked with a lot of people who are at that place in their lives. They know they've come off the straight and narrow, that they're not in God's will. Some have messed up their lives badly, some maybe as badly as I did. And I always tell them that the great thing about God is that if you call out to Him, if you don't give up, He will meet you right where you are and guide you back on course. Like the GPS in my car, once I admit I'm lost and push the help button, the voice comes on again and says, "I am rerouting you toward your destination."

The most amazing thing is that God rerouted me without condemnation. Yes, I still had regrets—many of them. But after I reset my life's compass toward Him, it didn't matter that the other roads in life were straighter or that they would've gotten me there faster. What mattered was that finally—*finally*—after years of wallowing with the pigs, I had come home.

And as I worked to clean up my life, it seemed God opened the store-houses of heaven and showered down blessings on me. Each gift, no matter how small, seemed like another ring, another robe, another fatted calf given to me by my heavenly Father, who wanted to welcome me joyfully back into His household. Life had gone so badly for so long that when things started looking up, I didn't take anything for granted. Even though my days proba-bly would have seemed pretty normal from most people's perspective, I thrived for days on each tiny blessing so that I felt like I was moving from mountaintop to mountaintop and cloud to cloud. When I woke up each morning fresh and alert in my apartment, I was as happy as if I had awakened at a five-star resort. Eating a drive-thru Egg McMuffin was like dining on eggs Benedict at the Ritz. Singing at a little country church was like singing at Carnegie Hall.

But far and away the most precious thing was mending my relationship with Megan. Each minute I spent with her was like watching a fresh morn-ing glory unfolding before my eyes. I remembered the night I'd looked down on myself and faced the awful possibility that my short, sorry life might end in an overdose, leaving for my daughter nothing but memories of an absen-tee dad who died a stinking, swollen addict. Now I was *so thankful* to have a second chance to be the father she deserved, to invest time in her and build for her a whole new set of memories of her daddy.

Meanwhile, my concerts started to become more spiritual. As I became more comfortable with sharing my story, it seemed that God brought the right people to hear it, whether I sang before hundreds or before fifty people crammed into a tiny room with a bad sound system. Years before I had dreaded small concerts and sometimes even considered them beneath me, a waste of time. But I remembered that all those years producers had driven me crazy, asking, "What do you have to say? What does Michael English have to say?"

Now I had plenty to say, and I knew that God wanted me to say it wherever He placed me.

I remember one small concert I did where, when I was singing "In Christ Alone," I looked down and saw a lone young man walk down the aisle and stand in front of the stage. *There's a story in him*, I thought, still singing. After the concert, I walked down and talked to him and learned he was dealing with the same addiction issues that had derailed me for so long. He'd climbed on the sobriety wagon several times and had always fallen off, just like me.

"I'm not sure I'm ever going to make it," he said.

I was overjoyed to be able to tell him what I had learned. "You've got to grab hold of God and let Him back into your heart!"

I was very careful not to paint a rosy picture, because my own healing had not been the Damascus Road type of experience, but one more like the prodigal son, who had to get all the way to the absolute bottom before his desperation drove him home. I had learned by then that instant healing was probably the exception, not the rule.

"I would love to be able to tell you that right after I turned my life over to God, everything was great," I told him. "But I ended up in a rehab center begging God to either help me or let me die. Let God be the strength in your weakness. You're not alone, not anymore. But you've got to make that step— turn it over to God and let Him start driving your life, because you'll crash and burn if you try to do it yourself."

I never found out what happened to that young man, but I know that I told Him what I'd promised God I would. And I was not ashamed.

+ chapter forty-seven +

Even through the worst times, I had remained friendly with Jackie's parents, Lloyd and Verna. One weekend in June 2002 they came to see me at a concert in Ohio, near where they lived. It was a two-night gig in a small school auditorium. To me, just to be booked was another blessing from God, and I was tickled to be there.

Before the show, I walked out from the green room to get a look at the crowd, and my path took me to the rear of the venue. As I turned to head backstage again, I caught a glimpse of a tall woman with short blond hair. Her back was to me, and she was walking out the back of the auditorium while talking on a cell phone. I couldn't see her face, only the sweep of her jaw where she held the phone. But there was something extremely familiar about her. I stopped in my tracks and watched her walk away.

During the concert, I scanned the crowd as I sang and spotted a few people I recognized, fans I'd met before and who traveled to see me when I performed in their area. But I didn't see the tall blond woman. After the show, I began working my way through the crowd toward the record table where I would be signing autographs. Usually people who want to chat with me will sort of fall into step beside me and start talking. But suddenly a tall figure emerged from the mass of people and stopped right in front of me. In fact, Marcie Stambaugh stopped everything. And when she spoke, it was like the whole crowd moving around me melted away and no one existed except her.

the prodigal comes home

"I don't know if you remember me . . . ," she began.

"Yes. Yes, I do remember you," I said.

I had met Marcie in Michigan and again in Idaho, but at that moment it was like I was seeing her for the first time. The thing I remember most of all about that moment is that even though she stood only five-nine to my six-four, I felt like I was looking up at her. She was so regal, so impressive. In my eyes, she was perfect.

It took me a few seconds to shake the stars out of my eyes, but eventually I was able to make the usual small talk. "How have you been?" *(Lonely,* I wanted to say. *How about you?)* "What have you been doing?" *(Kicking a nasty drug habit. How about you?)*

It turned out that Marcie had come to the concert with her friend Melissa again. We talked for a few moments about the last time we had seen each other, and I flashed back to her cutting up with Melissa in the front row at the Idaho fair, kicking back in my room with her shoes off, laughing and talking. As we stood there, I wished time would stop so that I wouldn't have to turn my attention to anyone else. But I knew I had to get to that record table.

"Hey, can you stick around for a few minutes?" I asked hopefully.

When she smiled, it was fresh and dazzling. "Sure. I'll be right over there with Melissa."

So Marcie and Melissa posted themselves against a wall a ways off. I signed autographs, flirted with Marcie from across the room, signed a few more autographs, flirted with her some more. After all the fans had gone their way, I walked over and invited both women to join me for dinner.

We wound up doing the same thing we'd done in Idaho, ordering take-out and eating around the table in my room at the Hampton Inn. There was no hand-holding between Marcie and me, no "Hey, let's start a romance." Still, I could feel an intensely special chemistry between us. Not just a physical attraction, but something deeper. I didn't do anything about it. Instead, the three of us just laughed and talked and watched a movie. Finally, it was time to go, and I walked them out to their car.

"Good night," Marcie said to me.

"Good night," I said. Then I closed her car door and watched them drive away.

Marcie and Melissa came to my show the next night, and we followed the same routine. Back in my room that night, though, I felt an anxiousness, knowing that when Marcie drove away this time, it would be all the way to Michigan. I could tell she felt the same way. The attraction was strong, deep, electric. Toward the end of the evening, we exchanged telephone numbers. And this time as they were leaving, I kissed Marcie good night.

Back in my room, I couldn't sleep. I was thirty-nine years old but felt eighteen. I kept tossing and turning, thinking about this bright, beautiful, fantastic woman who, I had learned, was a committed Christian and the daughter of a preacher. *What was going to happen? With her living so far away, could it even work?*

The next day I called her. I didn't want to seem overanxious, but I couldn't wait. We talked for an hour, then I told her I'd call her back that evening. I did, and we talked for an hour again. The next thing I knew, we were talking for an hour or two a couple of times a day. It seemed like we never ran out of things to say. She told me all about her family, and I told her about mine. She told me about her rebel days, and I told her about my struggle with addiction. I shared with her the miracle of the methadone program and let her know that I was still on it. We shared fears, hopes, disappointments, and dreams. Finally, we agreed we had to see each other again.

Marcie flew down to Nashville and stayed for four days. The time was glorious, another gift from God. I took her to as many of my favorite places as I could squeeze in. We went to the movies, she went with me to get my hair cut, and one afternoon we stayed home. Marcie loves to bake, so while I sat on the couch in the living room, she commandeered my kitchen and whipped up brownies and chocolate chip cookies from scratch. And for the first time ever, my tiny apartment smelled like home.

I thought, *This is the way it's supposed to be.*

Not that she was supposed to slave in the kitchen while I lounged on my butt on the couch! There was just this sense of peace, a *rightness* about her being there. With me. Us, together, passing time in a simple, sane, tranquil way.

Marcie and I became serious very quickly. Her story started coming out. She told me how she'd felt called to pray for me and that she had done so for three years. With a shyness unusual for her, she shared with me about the outrageous feeling she'd had that night in Michigan that she was supposed to marry me, and about how she'd prayed desperately for God to take that feeling away.

He didn't.

You have to understand that as a singer, I'd had proposals of marriage before. During my pop days, I received fan letters all the time from girls declaring their undying love. Once a woman even showed up at my manager's office wearing a wedding dress. But Marcie was different. As she told me how she felt, how she'd wrestled with it, how she'd gone on with her life and dated other men and nearly married, I began to think that maybe her feelings weren't as outrageous and ridiculous as she'd thought. I also realized that I was finally ready for a serious commitment.

+ chapter forty-eight +

Two months later, on August 29, 2002, we were married at the Tulip Street United Methodist Church in Nashville, a historic red-brick, stained-glass landmark built in 1892.

At first our wedding divided Marcie's family. Her mother, Cindy, and stepfather, Rich, supported us completely. Her siblings, Chad and Katie, were completely opposed to our getting married, as was her dad, Rev. Mike Stambaugh, who asked us to wait six months and see if we still felt the same way. In the end, I let Marcie decide. I could understand her father's feelings. From his point of view, his precious daughter was rushing headlong into a marriage with a divorced drug addict who had a court record, was still in treatment, and was seventeen years her senior. I didn't expect him to see it our way.

And he didn't. On our wedding day, as about seventy guests gathered in the church, Mike and Katie sat grimly in a corner of the sanctuary. Chad refused even to attend. Those memories are painful but understandable shadows on an otherwise perfect day.

Outside, a blue, late-summer day beamed sunlight through the antique stained glass, casting rainbows into the sanctuary. I stood at the altar and looked out at the guests. I was so happy to see Daddy and his new wife, Lena, along with a few old friends. Then suddenly I saw a pair of faces that flooded my heart with warmth: Norman Miller and his wife. I hadn't talked to

Norman or even seen him in years. I was touched that eight years after I blew apart his hard work, he still cared enough to come. I smiled at him, and he smiled back.

Topper Council performed the ceremony in his usual good-natured style. Megan was a bridesmaid, and her new boyfriend, Keith Cook, was an usher. (I didn't know then that I was looking at my future son-in-law; Megan and Keith would marry in 2005.) When Megan reached me, she stopped and gave me a great big kiss right on the mouth.

The way we'd planned things, I would sing "Love Moves in Mysterious Ways," a song from the *Hope* and *Healing* albums, as Marcie walked down the aisle. As I stood at the altar, I couldn't wait to see her in the dress I'd helped her pick out, a low-key, cream-colored creation that wrapped around her neck but left her tanned, elegant shoulders bare. Jay DeMarcus began playing the opening chords to "Love Moves," and Marcie appeared at the back of the church with her mom, who was to walk her down the aisle.

As soon as I saw her, I began to tremble. She was radiant, glowing in the soft natural light floating in through the stained glass. I've sung before tens of thousands of people in huge churches and concert halls, always standing there as solid as a rock, doing what I do. But now I was standing there in this church with fewer than a hundred people, and I was just . . . shaking.

Still, somehow, I was able to sing.

Love moves in mysterious ways.
It's always so surprising
When love appears over the horizon.
I'll love you for the rest of my days,
But still it's a mystery
How you ever came to me.
Which only proves
Love moves in mysterious ways.

When Marcie joined me at the front of the sanctuary, I felt like I was living a beautiful dream. As Murphy's Law would have it, though, the church air conditioner had broken, and I was perspiring like crazy in my tux. At one point right in the middle of the ceremony, Topper reached over and blotted my forehead with a small towel. Everyone laughed. Later in the ceremony, Jay, Missy, and Buddy Mullins sang. And when I kissed Marcie English for the first time, my heart swelled so big I thought it would pop the fancy buttons on my shirt.

We had our reception at Two Rivers Mansion, a gorgeous old 1870s home that you can rent for big events. My dad got up and made a little speech, telling the guests he was proud of the commitment we'd made to each other and welcoming Marcie into the family. As if that wasn't surprising enough, he then did something I never would have dreamed of in a thousand years: he danced with my wife. I was completely astonished.

My dad didn't wear shorts. He didn't approve of long hair. He didn't drink or play cards. And as a member in good standing of the North East Pentecostal Free Will Baptist Church, he never, ever, at any time, under any circumstances whatsoever, danced. Not even at a wedding.

I was so blown away by what I was seeing that I rushed around in the crowd tapping people on the shoulder and saying, "Look! My dad's dancing with my wife!"

I was so proud of him. Between his speech and the dancing, was the first moment I thought, *Hey, I've got the dad I've always wanted. A dad I can go to. A dad I can lean on.*

THE REST OF MARCIE'S FAMILY eventually warmed up to me. Through the next couple of years, as we spent time together at the holidays, Mike, Chad, and Katie gradually began to believe that I was a changed man and that I was crazy in love with Marcie. Then something happened that may have caused Mike's heart to thaw a little faster.

In September 2003, I was lying in bed early one morning—and I mean *early*, like about five o'clock—when I awoke to hear Marcie rustling around in the bathroom. I tried to stay awake and wait for her to come back to bed, but the next thing I knew, she was rousing me out of a sound sleep.

She looked about ready to burst with some kind of secret. "What is it?" I said sleepily.

"I was going to do this a different way and surprise you, but I'm so excited I can't help it. I'm pregnant!"

Instantly I was wide awake, laughing and on fire with the news. We started calling *everybody*, waking them all up at the crack of dawn to tell them. But about the time we'd gotten everyone told who needed telling, the look of the test started to bother me a little. The "positive" indicator was awfully faint.

"Are you sure you're really pregnant?" I asked Marcie.

"Yes, I'm sure," she said.

But I wasn't satisfied, so I jumped in the car and drove like a maniac to Kroger to buy more pregnancy tests at six o'clock in the morning.

Back home, I ripped open a two-pack and handed Marcie a fresh test. "Here. Take another one. I want to be sure."

"I *am* sure," she said.

"Just take another one . . . please. For me."

So she did, and it looked exactly like the first one, with the positive sign just barely showing. But Marcie was certain she was pregnant. "Michael, you wouldn't see anything at all if I wasn't," she said.

I still wasn't convinced. So while Marcie howled with laughter, I marched into the bathroom and took the other test myself. I *knew* I wasn't pregnant, and I wanted to see what a real negative looked like!

When absolutely nothing appeared on the positive part of the test, I shouted, "We're pregnant! We're going to have a baby!"

Less than nine months later, Isabella Grace English entered the world. And at that moment, life was absolutely perfect. My new baby girl was for me a symbol of purity. She had come from me, a formerly dirty, wretched man, and her coming meant to me that I had crossed over into a new phase of life. Bella's beauty seemed to outshine the darkness of all my failures.

For Bella's first year, I was Mr. Mom as Marcie worked ten-hour days as a debt collector to help make ends meet while I rebuilt my singing career. When Marcie was working and I had a gig, two good friends, Karen Russell and Christopher Lee Peters, stepped in and took care of Bella, earning the status of honorary aunt and uncle. Meanwhile, my friend Renee Barham tried to book as many concerts as she could, but we often struggled financially. During the years of my addiction, I had piled up a lot of bills, and they seemed to come due in waves.

During this time, Missy reacquainted me with a woman named Glenda McNalley, whom she knew from work connections. I had known Glenda years before when she worked for Norman. Through a series of conversations, she agreed to manage me, and I was grateful because I knew she believed I really had changed. Because of Glenda, my bookings began to increase. One of those, a concert at a Nashville church, was the beginning of still another round of healing.

+ chapter forty-nine +

I don't believe in coincidence, only in God's providence. That's why I think it was part of His plan that Glenda and Norman met for a business breakfast in August 2005.

"Have you seen Michael English recently?" Glenda asked Norman.

"Just at his wedding," Norman said. "Other than that, no."

Glenda shared a little bit about my recovery, my walk with God, and the brand-new life Marcie and I were building together. "You wouldn't believe how much Michael has changed," she said. "He's singing at a church in Nashville this weekend. Do you want to come see him?"

The way Norman tells it now, he sort of groaned inside. I didn't know this, but he had heard through the music grapevine now and again things like, "Michael's really changed! You should come see him!" Then the next thing he'd hear was that I'd been arrested or something.

So when Glenda came to him with a similar story, he was highly skeptical. But they were good friends, and he trusted her judgment more than the grapevine. That weekend he came with her to my concert and sat down in the back of the church, definitely not expecting any miracles. Then the guy who was emceeing made an announcement that, from Norman's point of view, made things even worse.

"I'm sorry to tell you this," the emcee said, "but Michael's got a bad sinus infection, and he won't be able to sing as many songs tonight. But he does have some things he wants to share from his heart."

Norman says now that he groaned inside even louder and thought, *This is going to be like purgatory.* Back when he was managing me, he'd always felt I did better onstage when I avoided talking and stuck to singing. But that night when I shared my story, Norman says he sat in his chair in disbelief. "Everything Michael said that night was either challenging, encouraging, inspiring, or funny," he tells people now. "It was unbelievable."

After the show, Norman came backstage and gave me a big hug. Megan was there, and she told him how great it was to have her daddy back.

"I'd love to have lunch with you," Norman said.

I told him that would be great. Late that night I sent him an e-mail. "Dear Norman," I wrote. "It was totally God who brought you there tonight. It's only His grace that would allow you to come after everything I've put you through. If you were serious about having lunch, I'd love to do that."

Norman says he was amazed to wake up the next morning and find that message waiting for him on his BlackBerry. The Michael English he knew never would have followed up so quickly, if at all. He called me at nine o'clock that morning and was shocked that his former client, the one who always slept until noon, had been up for four hours already.

"I get up every morning at five and make breakfast for Marcie," I told him. "She has to leave for work at six."

Norman says he thought to himself, *Who is this guy?*

He and I scheduled lunch. Then we got together for dinner with our wives. I don't know how it came up, but Norman mentioned the idea of our working together again. I was all for it, because in my opinion, he is the best manager in the business.

Still, Norman proceeded with caution and spent some time checking me out. Were these changes real or just a flash in the pan? First, he visited Lisa. She told him how, at Keith and Megan's wedding earlier that year, I'd apologized to her for all I'd put her through and thanked her for being such a good mother to Megan and for helping me through detox and rehab. Then she told Norman the story of how my cell phone battery died on the day

Megan and Keith were leaving for their honeymoon. Megan had said she would call Lisa and me, separately, from the airport to say good-bye. When I didn't hear from Megan, I called Lisa.

"Did Megan call you?" I asked.

"Yes."

"I think she called me too, but my cell battery died and I missed her call."

"That's okay," Lisa said, hearing how upset I was. "She's only going to be gone for a week. You can talk to her when she gets back."

"No, that's not good enough," I told her. "I've already missed so much in her life, and I don't want to miss another moment ever again."

Of course, when I told Lisa that, I had no idea anyone but her would ever hear it. But to Norman's ears it was more confirmation that I was a different man. He also talked to my pastor, Stan Mitchell, senior pastor of GracePointe Church. Stan told Norman how I'd made myself personally accountable to him in a way that I had refused to do when I was singing solo.

These conversations took place within a month of Norman's first coming to hear me at that Nashville church. He later told me, "I have never seen such a change in a person in my life."

And that's why a man with as great a reputation in Christian music as Norman Miller agreed to manage me again. At first industry people thought he was crazy. But slowly they've come around. Glenda bowed out graciously, more concerned that I continue on a healing path than with her own interests. I'm very grateful to her. If she had not been in my life, Norman and I might never have reunited.

Just as he had when he took over my career in 1991, Norman immediately made things happen. We began collecting songs for a new album. We started working on a pilot for a new, upgraded version of *The Michael English Show* for TBN. By early 2006, Marcie was able to quit work and stay home with Bella. Megan's husband, Keith, became my road manager. Today I stay busy singing—and having something to say.

Five years into my recovery from hardcore drug addiction, I still see my doctors for treatment and counseling. And I get letters all the time from people who tell me they're glad I'm talking about it, because it helps them

the prodigal comes home

know they're not alone. I want people to know that even though God doesn't always deliver the Damascus Road miracle, that even though the road back home can be winding and rough, our heavenly Father walks with us and welcomes us home with open arms.

+ chapter fifty +

It's amazing how much things have changed with my earthly father. Even after I was grown, my home was always a negative, glass-half-empty place. But over the past couple of years, Daddy and I have both grown older and wiser. Our relationship is turning into a completely different one, and I cherish it.

The other day we were talking, and Daddy said, "By the way, have you talked to your mother?"

The question scared me. He had never asked me that. Never ever.

"No. Why?"

"I'm a little worried about her," Daddy said. "She's not talking as plain as I'm used to her talking. She came out and kept up the store for a few hours the other day, and I couldn't make out what she was saying."

In years past, Daddy wouldn't have given a plug nickel to understand what Mama was saying, or if he did, he wouldn't have said so. I wanted to tell him that I was used to him being the negative one in the family, but I'll be doggoned if he didn't say exactly what I was thinking.

"Used to be I was the one who was negative," he said.

That may seem small to some people, but for us it was a revelation. Then he said, "Son, I just want you to know how much I love you and how much I appreciate our relationship."

My heart nearly flew out of my body. I couldn't figure out whether to hold the receiver out and stare at it like some kind of strange science specimen or hug it close to my chest like something precious that was lost but now is found. So I just said, "Daddy, you have no idea how much I feel the same way."

It was an astonishing conversation. The healing of this oldest of wounds has taught me that there's hope for just about anything. I've been told that time and age change people, that if a man is hard and bitter, he can get softer with age. I just knew my dad was going to be the exception to that rule. For a time, it seemed like I would be proven a genius: the older he got, the more ornery he got. But in the last couple of years, he has turned into a teddy bear. And maybe he's not the only one.

It used to be that whenever I talked to Daddy, the ugly past sat on my shoulder and whispered bad memories into my ear. Now, it's as though one conversation with him kind of erases five years of pain.

My relationship with God has changed too. The God I thought I knew as a child and, really, for most of my adult life was a lot like Daddy used to be: stern, ready to blame and punish. I didn't learn much at all about grace and mercy. I grew up thinking that if you were in a backslidden state, you were going to hell. And when I was a raging addict, short of killing somebody, I could have slid no farther back. I had no hope.

But from what I've seen over the past few years, I've had to reconsider. It's now hard for me to believe that a God who loves me so much, who has poured out His healing mercies into my life, would have rejected me at my lowest point. Isaiah writes that God sees the end from the beginning. That means He knew I also thirsted for righteousness, longed for it, reached for it, but could not find it within myself to grab hold of it. He knew I would come running back to Him and that He would greet me with rings and feasts. How then could the same God have sent me to hell had a car hit me while I was on a drug buy?

That is something I still wrestle with, and I know there are whole camps of preachers who are way smarter than me dug in like armies on each side of this debate. As a recently reformed semiprofessional sinner, I'm not going to pretend to make some profound statement here on a centuries-old debate. But I will say that my own experience with a patient and loving God has me thinking hard about it. At the very least, I know this: we always have hope.

It's not like I got hold of some good theology somewhere and now I understand everything. It's more like I'm at that place where a lot of new Christians are—seeking and hungry. I can't stand to lie in bed anymore. I want to get up! I want to see what God's got cooking every day, because I know it's going to be good. And when I lay my head on the pillow again each night, I can rest well in Him, knowing that finally, after all my wandering, my heart is back at home.

+ notes +

Chapter 18

1. Bill Gaither with Ken Abraham, *It's More Than the Music: Life Lessons on Friends, Faith, and What Matters Most* (New York: Warner Faith, 2003), 2.

2. Ibid.

3. Ibid.

+ acknowledgments +

The Bible states in Matthew 18:20: "Where two or three are gathered together in my name, there am I in the midst of them." This project was made possible through the combined efforts of people who share the same love for Christ as I do.

This book would not have been written without the vision and persistence of Norman Miller. He has believed in me more than I believed in myself.

Lynn Vincent assisted in bringing my story to life in a way I couldn't have done on my own. Lynn, you saved this project!

The team at Thomas Nelson has consistently supported me since the inception of this project. Their passion has given me more than they could ever imagine.

There are a few more people who brought this to fruition. Everyone in life has a mentor, someone they look up to and respect—mine is Bill Gaither.

I could not continue on my journey without the accountability and counsel of my pastor and friend Stan Mitchell.

Missy Council has been with me through all the rough times, and thank God she is enjoying the good times. My memory wasn't always clear, so I am thankful for her clarity.

Finally, my family—for allowing me to share their lives in order to tell my story. I love you all.